DATE		

Meaning and Signs in Fiction

MEANING AND SIGNS IN FICTION

Alan Kennedy

ST. MARTIN'S PRESS NEW YORK

ISBN 0–312–52380–7

Library of Congress Cataloging in Publication Data

Kennedy, Alan.
   Meaning and signs in fiction.
   Includes index.
   1.   English fiction--History and criticism.
I. Title.
PR826.K4   823′.03   78-24284
ISBN 0-312-52380-7

TO WALTER ALLEN

Contents

Preface

Pound's challenge to poetry and poets is 'make it new'. It is, to say the least, a sobering thought to have ringing in one's ears when setting out on the well-worn paths that lead one to Dickens, Jane Austen, George Eliot, Joseph Conrad and others that are discussed in this book. The novel, as D. H. Lawrence so well said, is the one bright book of life. The novelty, the life, the brightness of the novel require not only constant renewal from novelists, but also fresh experience by readers. Readers must actively construct anew for themselves the meaning of fictions. This does not mean that the meanings they construct and their experiences are necessarily different on the whole from the meanings and experiences of previous readers. It must be possible to make it new without making it radically different in kind. Whether or not it succeeds in doing so, this book tries to meet that challenge. It tries to do this, in part, by assuming that all novels are contemporary—contemporary, that is, with the reader. This is the same thing, of course, as saying that they are timeless, or saying that they are 'poetic' constructions that, when activated by a reader, speak beyond the limits of the time of their production by an author. It would be inaccurate, therefore, to speak only of continuities in the novels here considered. The patterns are more like spontaneous recurrences. The central event that gives rise to these recurrences is the novelist's recurrent need to structure meaning in signs. In one particular sense, then, this book is an attempt at a structural history of the novel, although it is more accurately a first try at a history of the way meaning is structured in the novel.

It happens that questions of meaning, signification, and structure are amongst the most important and controversial questions of this time. This fact has one particular advantage here, in that it facilitates the attempt to read 'traditional' fiction as contemporary fiction. It should be added that while the topics of this book come close to topics studied by 'structuralists', I am not one of their number and have no expertise or training in their field of study. What I know of the subject I have picked out of the air—and a few books—as we all do. Saul Bellow's Herzog says that '"Humankind lives mainly upon perverted ideas"'. He suggests that any philosopher '"who wants to keep his contact with mankind should pervert his own system in advance to see how it will really look a few decades after adoption"'. Structuralists will probably welcome me in this role of perverter of their ideas. Perhaps they themselves have already taken Herzog's advice. In any case, the reader can be reassured that he will need no specialised knowledge of 'structuralism' in order to read the following account of fiction.

Meaning, significance, structure are topics too important to be left to the 'experts'. What I have tried to do is to allow another neglected group of experts, novelists, to speak for themselves on these matters. Many of the general ideas and conclusions may seem to be counter to received opinion of our times. The ideas will be seen to be justified, if at all, by the degree to which they are seen to be appropriate as ways to renew experience of the novels themselves.

Some of the chapters can be read as independent essays on individual novelists, but there is some advantage in reading the book as a whole. Concepts that are used throughout are developed in the first chapters. Ideas developed in one chapter are often quietly echoed in a later one, so that there is a cumulative—and sometimes, inevitably, a repetitive—effect. Virtually all the notes at the end are non-substantive, consisting primarily of page references for quotations. Because I am tracing quite closely a series of related metaphors over a wide range, I have felt it necessary to give such references in order to allow the reader to have a look for himself. For the most part I have used inexpensive paperbacks to which the average reader will have ready access. The book does not really carry its analysis right up to modern writers, although the conclusion deals briefly with the twentieth century. Space was one consideration in this. The other is that I have already dealt with very similar matters in *The Protean Self: Dramatic Action in Contemporary Fiction.*

The book is dedicated to Walter Allen partly because he suggested that themes from the earlier book could be usefully applied to traditional fiction. It is dedicated to him primarily because of the work he has done for literature.

I am grateful to my colleagues Mike Klug and Bruce Stovel for reading parts of the manuscript and giving me the benefit of their opinions. Thanks to Colleen Clattenburg for speed and accuracy and long hours in typing.

I am also grateful to Laura Riding for permission to reproduce her poem 'Because of Clothes', from *The Collected Poems of Laura Riding.*

Much of Chapter 4 appeared in Volume III, Number 2 of *English Studies in Canada.*

Dalhousie University   A.K.
July 1977

Because of Clothes

Without dressmakers to connect
The good-will of the body
With the purpose of the head,
We should be two worlds
Instead of a world and its shadow
The flesh.

The head is one world
And the body is another—
The same, but somewhat slower
And more dazed and earlier,
The divergence being corrected
In dress.

There is an odour of Christ
In the cloth: below the chin
No harm is meant. Even, immune
From capital test, wisdom flowers
Out of the shaded breast, and the thighs
Are meek.

The union of matter with mind
By the method of raiment
Destroys not our nakedness
Nor muffles the bell of thought.
Merely the moment to its dumb hour
Is joined.

Inner is the glow of knowledge
And outer is the gloom of appearance.
But putting on the cloak and cap
With only the hands and the face showing,
We turn the gloom in and the glow forth
Softly.

Wherefore, by the neutral grace
Of the needle, we possess our triumphs
Together with our defeats
In a single balanced couplement:
We pause between sense and foolishness,
And live.

Laura Riding

1 Significant Action and Cannibal Clothes

For books are not absolutely dead things, but do contain a potency of life in them to be as active as that soul was whose progeny they are; nay, they do preserve as in a vial the purest efficacy and extraction of that living intellect that bred them.

Areopagitica

The belief that books are somehow active and infused with the intended meaning (or soul) of their authors is not a new one, as the passage from Milton shows. In fact, the belief that in reading a text—especially a fictional or poetic text—we are in communication with the personality of the author is a belief now so out of date as to deserve to be called old-fashioned. The 'intentional fallacy' argument (that an author's 'real' or original intention is irrecoverable from the text itself) dealt the first blow to this old-fashioned belief in the personal communicativeness of art and the structuralist study of texts is dealing the second. For the structuralists the personal element is beneath notice. The author has become the medium and language itself, or society, has become the author. Structuralists are interested in the way in which systems—systems of signs, or of economics, or of social structure—imprint themselves on individual texts despite the author's personal intent. From this point of view, the individual writer or reader of a text can be nothing but passive. The text writes its own author and creates its own reader.[1] Fashionable as such notions currently are, they too have quite a history and writers have probably always paid tribute either to afflatus or inspiration.[2] Intelligent readers have also discovered that the books they read and re-read often seem to understand them better than they understand the books. Milton's claim, of course, contains also this idea of passivity in the reference to the 'potency of life in them' which suggests the potentiality, as of a foetus, that will be active soon, but not yet. Books are 'not absolutely' dead things. Milton, however, in his old-fashioned way, has the emphasis right, on activity. And it is the emphasis one makes, or the assumptions one operates with, that are crucial to the degree of understanding one can achieve by analysis. To assume the passivity of the text is to blind oneself to a whole range of perceptions and meanings. In spite of the truth that there is an element of passivity in literature (a truth that will not be ignored below), it is essential at this time to re-assert the activity—the significant activity—of fiction.

The central force of this claim—that the novel is significantly active in the world—is in opposition to the view that the novel is the bourgeois romantic epic, reflecting (passively, not critically) middle-class values and ultimately pandering to a middle-class desire for the quiet life. It denies, that is to say, that the novel is an insignificant and passive presence in the world. Similarly, the present argument will assert that characters in novels are not merely sentimental characters educated into accepting (again passively) a pre-defined position in established society. Characters in novels will be seen to grow towards an active engagement with their situations. Indeed, this is exactly what significant activity is. One can, of course, be active without being consciously and critically aware of the context (personal, social, historical) in which one acts. Although on such occasions we pay lip service of the 'out of the mouths of babes' variety to the fact that naive and uninformed activity may by some fluke of 'genius' be appropriate, it can be seen that on most occasions such activity will be insignificant; it won't count. Inversely, one may have a highly developed perceptive faculty, as well as accurate judgement and highly sensitive feelings, and maybe even philosophical expertise at one's subjective command. All of this personal potential will go for nought, however, if it is never realised in action. Its significance will be passive, and will ultimately atrophy. Significant action, then, results only from the interaction of subjectivity and objectivity.

The structural paradigm for all significant action in fiction comes from language itself; or, more precisely, from the active attempt to use language significantly. The meaning the writer feels he has within him as potential requires acting out in language in order to be fully significant. This significant action requires from the writer a peculiar degree of passivity. He cannot make the language do what it is not capable of doing; he must passively align himself with the fact that the ground of his action is given. If he does not, his action will remain insignificant because it is incommunicable. It will not exist in signs. Conversely, if he is merely passive, he will find that the language will betray him. He will use clichés, or dead or hollow expressions that will not convey exactly what he wishes to convey. Many novels—by means of what could be called the 'dyer's hand hypothesis'—show internal evidence of the author's necessary struggle with the forms of language. Some characters seem to exist only to give expression to the author's love of expression (Felix Holt's powerful ability as a speaker is an example of this). A character's struggle to make his own sense of the world significantly active in his own society is a transformation of the original struggle with the medium of language on the part of the author. The activity of writer, or character, turns out paradoxically to be a kind of passive activity, if it is significant. The paradoxical nature of fiction needs no stressing; it arises from the fact that fiction attempts to express the inexpressible. So it should not be surprising that fiction seeks to define a paradoxically passive action. The paradox seeks to point to a middle term that has been excluded by a dialectical pair. Coleridge indicates the pair of terms appropriate to the present discussion in the following passage:

Few and unimportant would the errors of men be, if they did but know, first what they themselves mean: and secondly, what the *words* mean by which they attempt to convey their meaning.[3]

The interaction of these two meanings—which might be referred to as 'my meaning' and the 'world's meaning'—is dramatic and is itself the structural origin of the novel's continual fascination with the drama, another topic which is to be developed throughout this book. Owen Barfield develops the comment from Coleridge by differentiating between 'speaker's meaning' and 'lexical meaning'. Lexical, or dictionary meaning is the fixed or fossilised, mechanical, world's meaning. Poetry arises from the infusion of speaker's meaning into the lexical meaning. The rigid form of language is hollow and must be filled from the inside by the meaning of the speaker. Similarly the meaning of the speaker is not fully in the world until it is incarnated in words by an act of realisation. Barfield speaks of the pair of polar opposites 'expression' and 'communication' as coinciding in the poetic text (what I am calling the 'significant act'). Although the terms appear to be mutually exclusive, so that the more one expresses oneself the less will be communicated and vice versa, the essential relationship between the pairs is not, he says, quantitative but *dynamic*:

This means that, though each of them is exclusive of, or counter to, the other, yet they are both concurrently necessary. They are, so to speak, 'sweet enemies.' And it is in this polarity that the depths of language are to be found. The two functions conflict, but they also co-operate. You can say, if you like, that the concern of communication is with the *how*, whereas the concern of expression is with the *what*. Perfect communication would occur if all words had and retained identical meanings every time they were uttered and heard. But it would occur at the expense of expression. In the same way, perfect individual or personal expression can only be achieved at the expense of communication, or at all events, at the expense of accuracy in communication.[4]

The active imagination expresses itself into the recalcitrant forms of language and the resultant creation is composite of polar opposites. The poetic text, then, is both expressive act and communicative fact; the action is suspended in the passive forms and the whole thing can become vital once again only by means of the interpretive activity of a reader, who must see beyond the surface forms to the informing sense. The implication of this fact is that the relationship of reader to text is also dynamic.

Earlier, mention was made of the possibility that passive text produced passivity in the reader. This was a loose way of putting the matter. One could say, in fact, that to the extent to which a text actively contains one meaning that it presents to the world, the reader is passive; he must be receptive to the message, the communication. This is the usual definition of a 'classic'. Certain current attitudes reverse this relationship; for instance Frank Kermode in *The Classic* appears to argue that the 'classic' is that text which is richly passive in face of the active interpreter. Every generation finds its own meaning by interpreting in its own terms what the text 'means'. The 'classic' is the text which by one means or another contrives to be passive to the greatest number of successive generations of interpreters. Both these positions are denied by arguing that neither text nor reader is either wholly passive or active. In fact, the reader and the text are composed of those polar opposites: passivity and activity. Like writing, the art of reading or interpreting is a passive activity, or an active passivity. Unless we assume that the apparently objective and passive text has within it, as it were, an active subjectivity, we shall be misreading—and misreading is not a creative act, it is an offence against the 'sovereign ghost'.

The subjectivity of the text is not immediately accessible to us however. It is only *mediately* available to us, by means of signs, which require interpreting. Now, the implication of all of this is that amongst readers there will be different interpretations, and at the same time there will be general agreement as to what a text seems to mean. A classic, since we shall continue to have to use the term, is the text which means more than the words can contain; it means more than the words literally say. It speaks universally to all, and individually to each one; it is general and particular. A reader, by way of the surfaces of the signs, feels himself in touch with a 'meaning' which he cannot fully express except by pointing to the text itself. The subjective activity of the reader or interpreter will be significant in so far as it tests itself against the objectivity of the signs of the text; it must be related to its ground or be dismissed as overactive insignificance. Similarly, an inactive literal 'reading' of the text will not amount to a significant activity. One must always read beyond or between the lines. The most reassuring thing about these comments is that they square with what most intelligent readers and critics have always said about reading literature. They amount, that is to say, to a re-assertion of the common reader's beliefs about literature. One might be distressed at the lack of originality of an idea, but the validity of the thought is perhaps confirmed by seeing that it agrees with what most people think.

Writing, reading, speaking, then, are difficult activities precisely because they are mediated. The poet's struggle is to make the passive matter of the language coincide with the spirit of his meaning. As was suggested above, this tension or polarity is dramatic, and is the source of the novel's fascination with the drama. Shortly we shall consider how some of these ideas emerge from Shakespeare. Brice Parain confirms what has been said about the nature of the speaker's relationship to language in the following:

Despite the monist prejudices of today . . . I see two faces to our consciousness, one turned outward which speaks and one linked with the most obscure of our personal, internal peculiarities which goes down to some roots there. I assume rather than am able to verify this one's existence because I have never been able to isolate it completely. But I know that not everything in us is reducible to language and that there is a part of us that seems to be silent and even resists language as freedom resists slavery. It is that part of us that is apparent in those unexpected, slightly foolish moments that overtake us.[5]

Further, and more to our purpose: 'To speak is an effort; it provokes disquiet; in short, it is work and too serious to be done easily. On the other hand, this duplicity is good. It is dramatic.'[6] What the novel does is to attempt to differentiate this essential duplicity from an inessential one that looks like it. The drama of confrontation of private and public, in language or in society, is an essential duplicity. One must be an *actor* in public, but this drama is good because it is significant. The freedom of our private reverie, which as Parain so aptly notes is often merely foolish, becomes significant freedom—or freedom under the law—only by enacting itself in public, mediately. Thought is only significant when it puts on the clothing of language. The danger is that the clothes will be mistaken for thought itself. Which is to say that another fundamental concern of the novel, that can be seen to arise from the structural matrix of the active use of language by the author, is the possibility of hypocrisy.

But we must back up briefly to mention the importance of the thought of Kenneth Burke, which becomes essential as soon as one begins to describe the world in dramatic terminology. Two fundamental principles of Burke's are relevant. The first is his dictum: 'Things move, people act.' The second is the fact that man is in essence a symbol user. When he does act, he acts in the field of his symbol system, and so it is possible to describe human nature as that which engages in 'symbolic action', or activity in, by and with symbols. Men can be moved of course, but the belief that people act suggests that humanity is only 'full' when free activity is possible. This free activity is obviously never unmediated; it is always presented to the world in some terminology or other. The interplay between intention and completed act is dramatic and for this reason the dramatic metaphor (as Burke argues in *Permanence and Change*, and elsewhere) is the most fundamental and profound metaphor available for us in attempting to account for human nature. It ought to be, then, that the history of the novel will reveal a recurrent interest in the drama, not only for literary historical reasons, but for what must be called structural ones. Whenever a fiction focuses on the interaction of several figures over any length of time and when, therefore, matters of signification are in evidence, there is bound to be a necessary recurrence of interest in the dramatic problems that centre around the subject of embodying meaning in symbols.

We know, from the linguistics of Ferdinand de Saussure and from the many semiotic studies deriving from him, that the relationship between the signifier and the signified is an arbitrary one. There is no necessary reason why any visual or oral symbols need carry one meaning. Indeed many identical sounds can convey one or many meanings. Syntax often serves to single out for us what particular 'signified' is intended, and so does context. Ambiguity is hard to avoid all the time, however. Here, then, is a central matter in the study of signification. In terms of the novel, several narrative possibilities derive from this fact of language, that is, from its arbitrariness. The first possibility is that language does work, particularly poetic language; all arbitrariness is overcome and the characters present themselves fully in their words: intention and sign coincide. Alternatively, there may be misinterpretation of the signs. A character may have a particular nature, as does Tom Jones say, but because of the tricksiness of signs he can be, and is, misrepresented and misinterpreted. The action of the novel (*Tom Jones*) then works towards a realignment of signified and signifiers. The two opposites to the previous situations are both contained in the single situation of hyprocrisy. The hyprocrite is possible only because of the arbitrariness of signs; he relies on misinterpretation, even though he intends the interpretation received when he is successful in his presentation. The intention of the hyprocrite is a surface one only; it is in a sense a hollow intention. He intends a manipulation of the surface of signifiers so as to suggest that, possibly, he is a trustworthy man when in fact he is not. In this case the signifier is hollow. It does its job and yet if one could somehow see beneath the surface of the hyprocrite, see below the costume he wears to put on his act, one would find an absolute discrepancy between signifier and signified. The novel often is concerned with cases of mistaken identity and its action often attempts to set up ways in which the hollow word can be differentiated from the full one. Because one of its fundamental principles is that men act in symbols, and that they must engage in symbolic action or be incomplete, the novel must often recur to the question of hyprocrisy (which is a term deriving originally from the stage). Further, it is clear that relatedness in novels is primarily a matter of interpretation between individuals. Love is a stage of relatedness at which words (or signs) become meaningful.

The argument thus far has suggested that certain forms of fiction are inherent in language itself; or rather, to be more precise, that the active *use* of language offers us analogues to what we find in fiction. It is in the interaction between what I have called 'intention', or signified, and the forms of language that the tension is originated that informs the novel. Continental structuralists, particularly Tzvetan Todorov,[7] have argued that the forms of language themselves give rise to the forms of fiction. This I take to be a passive theory of derivation—or a theory of passive derivation. The forms of fiction, according to this passive theory, are merely the forms of language writ large. This kind of structuralist thought is not one I wish to be thought to be allied with—unless, as is very possible, I misinterpret it. Although language is made by men, it is not made by individual men, and the pre-structuring attitude inherent in Todorov's suggestion seems to leave out what I take to be all-important: the necessary activity on the part of the author who is attempting to signify. In arguing that the novel reveals a structural consistency, I mean to suggest that because the situation in which men attempt to act significantly, or to act by signifying, is one which recurs identically over and over, there is bound to be some evidence of different individuals having achieved the same use of 'elements' of structure in their work. Todorov's idea is a very suggestive one nevertheless. The periodic sentence, for instance, in which ultimate predication is delayed until near the very end of the sentence, could well be thought to be an originating form for some forms of fiction. The story of *Oedipus Rex* is obviously the story of a life told in the form of a periodic sentence, as is the story of *Tom Jones*. It is not because we are subject to a structuring tendency on the part of language, however, that we find that human history has produced similar forms. The structural similarities arise from the fact that men always, because of their active nature, attempt to create structures of signification. Such structures are achieved, rather than imposed.

There is a cluster of situations and attitudes that can be derived, up to a point, by means of a deductive analysis of the nature of language use. Only by means of particular analytic investigation will the point become fully clear, and I mean shortly to turn to particular poetic structures for analysis. Before getting into extended analysis, however, it might be useful to suggest briefly how 'significant action' occurs in a few works. Richardson's *Clarissa* is the story of a pure but misrepresented soul, who suffers because of the plots of the arch-hyprocrite, Lovelace. Lovelace's extremely active use, or misuse, of signals turns out ultimately to be insignificant in the face of the apparently passive but ultimately more effectively active soul of Clarissa Harlowe. This novel will be considered in more detail in Chapter 3, but one might just note in passing that the essential goal of envisioning the unity of the private and social sides of character in the novel is here split into two. Clarissa is pure soul, misrepresented by society. For the nineteenth-century novel, soul is seen as something which grows, which evolves and requires both education (drawing out) and culture. This growing soul must itself struggle with the medium of representation and is itself often responsible—because of a lack of projective activity—for its own misunderstanding. The Clarissa version of purity misrepresented by forces outside its control does not disappear of course, as is evidenced by Collins' *The Woman in White* which is another study in the way in which the hypocritical villain (Fosco) manipulates surface appearances in order to betray the pure soul (of Laura), by representing her to be the insane woman in white, Anne Catherick. Based at least in part on the premise that 'crime causes its own detection', *The Woman in White* shows how a deep concern for the Truth, and for Innocence, will ultimately prevail against theatrical manipulation of surface appearance. Along the way there may well be disasters, but they contrive to happen to dispensable characters like Anne Catherick. Laura suffers a brief and traumatic (but not lasting or permanently damaging, we may imagine) incarceration in a madhouse, but the novel ends when the proper detective work has been done by Walter Hartright. Walter, as his name indicates, finds meaning below the surface, in the heart, and he struggles to make this deep meaning come to the top in order to rewrite the appearance of things. The novel ends symbolically with the erroneous writing on the tombstone being chipped off and the proper writing being inscribed in its place. Correct writing is possible, it turns out, and the theatrical hypocrisy of such as Fosco can be overcome by active attention both to the surface clues and to what cannot yet be seen.

By contrast, Mr F's aunt, in *Little Dorrit*, has had her heart go wrong at some time, and therefore, as violently active as she sometimes is in her insane speechifying, she never makes any sense. So little does she signify as a human being, that at one point she is in danger of being made into meat pies—just one instance of Dickens's interest in cannibalism; having lost that which gives language significance, Mr F's aunt is just so much meat. Flora Casby, whose mistake it is to try to make dead romance appear on a new stage, has a deeply confused and silly heart and therefore her syntax is out of control. As the impulses of her heart have become confused, lost somewhere between past and future, so they have lost projective power and language itself seems to have caught her up and is rolling her through the rest of her days like a juggernaut. Mrs Clennam is very significant in terms of the story in that she has tremendous effect on the lives around her. She is active only in a wilful or mechanical sense, however, and her ultimate inactivity of soul is indicated by her paralysis. It is only when the frozen sea within her is thawed by Little Dorrit that she becomes a full human being again, briefly, and moves from her wheelchair. The apparently passive Dorrit is revealed to be capable of a greater activity after all. The pattern for this type of insignificantly active character (like Mrs Clennam) seems to have been created by Jane Austen, especially in the figure of Mrs Norris in *Mansfield Park*. Her spirit of activity is that of a superficial busybody, and when really called on to act significantly she is paralysed. Emma, one might say, is a benign version of Mrs Norris, one who does have the potential for sensible development. Her overactivity, in matchmaking and imagining, is inappropriate to the setting in which she finds herself and is therefore, at the least, insignificant—although certainly productive of error, misunderstanding and pain. Fanny Price, on the other hand, is capable of accurate judgement and has an inner significance, but she is too inactive; she does not project her significance into the world. Anne Elliott, whose word has no weight, is similar.

Conrad's Lord Jim moves from a state of passivity, or paralysis caused by excessive imaginative activity, to a condition of vital activity in Patusan. On the training ship, the activity of his imagination seems to blind him to the real situation outside him, the potential ground of activity, and so cripple him for significant action. Because Jim has something of value inside him, Conrad and Marlow are willing to suspend belief in the value of a fixed code of conduct and follow Jim into the world of his second chance, a world dominated by suggestions of a dreamlike, subjective quality; as if, even if Jim were to succeed in Patusan in proving himself, somehow the achievement would be still potential, not, somehow, having occurred in the real, or public, world. The whole of his heroic achievement in Patusan is indeed clouded by the doubt that it is insignificant, that it does not count because in a sense he has not yet worked in the ranks. One must remember that the special friend who says to Marlow that one must work in the ranks or one's life doesn't count is a racist. He believes that giving one's life up to them, '(*them* meaning all of mankind with skins brown, yellow, or black in colour) "was like selling your soul to a brute"'. He contends further that relationship with *them* is ' "only endurable and enduring when based on a firm conviction in the truth of ideas racially our own, in whose name are established the order, the morality of an ethical progress"'. To all of which Marlow offers the enigmatic comment 'Possibly!' One significance, in this context, of Jim's life is the implicit defeat of racism that it represents. He stands before the court of his peers after the Patna affair, but clearly his appearance is intended as a denial of the authority of that court. Brierly seems to read this implied message and commits suicide, presumably having seen the flaw in the system to which he has been loyal. By contrast, Jim presents himself to Doramin, after the death of Dain Waris, and again apparently passive as he accepts the judgement, one can sense that he actively affirms Doramin's right to judge him. The court of *them* is proved to be as deserving of respect—perhaps more deserving—than that of civilised Europe. The nagging doubt that surrounds Jim's life is not forgotten even at the moment when he may be morally affirming the unity of mankind, however. We are reminded that he may still be betraying both himself, and the love of Jewel—who believes him to have been false, to have run away from her—for a shadowy ideal of conduct.

Racism is an important subject in *Lord Jim*, as it is in *Heart of Darkness*. Marlow, in *Heart of Darkness*, reluctantly begins to admit his common humanity with the howling savages of the jungle. Jim, with little apparent reluctance, affirms this common humanity, and judges himself guilty when he breaks faith with humanity and causes the death of Dain Waris. All this is very fine, but the claim of the privileged friend has an insistent truth about it. Jim's life, in itself, is insignificant; it doesn't count because it is not Doramin who needs to learn a lesson about racism; it is not Doramin who needs to have his common humanity demonstrated to him. Jim's moral activity would only have significance if performed in Europe; that is the ground on which—or the medium by means of which—one has to demonstrate the universality of humanity. The irony of Jim's life, of course, is that that is precisely the ground which has been cut from under him. His act is insignificant then because it occurs in the wrong setting, on the wrong stage. It is left to Conrad, and Marlow, to give Jim's meaning significance. It is Marlow who completes, or realises Jim's meaning by telling, like the ancient mariner, the story in Europe. Under the pressure of the elusive meaning of Jim's life, Marlow, like Jim, is tormented into 'a meticulous precision of statement [that] would bring out the true horror behind the appalling face of things', and Conrad, having caught a glimpse of Jim's original, says that 'It was for me, with all the sympathy of which I was capable, to seek fit words for his meaning.' Marlow's (and Conrad's) words would have no significance were it not for that intuition of the hidden life (the sovereign ghost) to which they point and direct our attention; and the ghost could never be actual were it not for the words.

It is not surprising to find novelists concerned with action and passion. Not all, however, show the kind of philosophical concern about the implications of this pair of terms for identity and society as does someone like Conrad, or like George Eliot, who offers the following bit of theatrical dialogue as a lead-in to Chapter 64 of *Middlemarch*:

> 1st Gent.   Where lies the power, there let the blame lie too.
> 2nd Gent.   Nay, power is relative; you cannot fright
>   The coming pest with border fortresses,
>   Or catch your carp with subtle argument.
>   All force is twain in one: cause is not cause
>   Unless effect there be; and action's self
>   Must needs contain a passive. So command
>   Exists but with obedience.

Not of least interest is the dramatic form of the passage, for Eliot is aware that an interest in activity is in itself an interest in dramatic action. *Daniel Deronda* and *Middlemarch* are studies in the meaning of significant action, which is action that has an effect. The philosophical problems of cause and effect need to be quietly circumvented if we are to get the point. Unless there is some visible public impact on environment (or scene, or stage), then there has been no 'action' in the sense Eliot seems to be trying to define. A productive passivity in action arises from taking the environment of one's activity into account. One must be passive in order to perceive clearly what is taking place outside of one's imagination. Only with realistic clarity of perception of the otherness of the grounds of one's action is there a chance for that action to be significant. Gwendolen Harleth of *Daniel Deronda* is highly active, theatrically active, but she is doomed to ineffectuality and insignificance because she is blind to the real state of affairs in which she moves. In fact, she is often wilfully blind, choosing not to understand her situation, as in the matter of the warning given her by Lydia Glasher. In *The Portrait of a Lady* Isabel Archer, who is modelled on Gwendolen, learns how to make her life significant, for Pansy, by actively choosing a life of passivity as wife of Osmond. Indeed, James's America-Europe theme could be schematised using our present terminology. America offers energetic actors without a stage suitable for their best acts, while Europe offers, by contrast, a highly active stage (or cultural setting) in which the actors have become mere reflex activities of the stage or setting itself. They are trapped into the passivity of a role. The James story finds its genesis in the interaction of vital actor and vital, but alien setting (with the occasional reversal as in *The Europeans*). To return to Eliot, Daniel Deronda is a character of great potential significance, but he is not fully active until he encounters Mordecai and discovers a historical stage appropriate to the completion of the personal motives being born in him. These topics will be discussed further in the following chapters, but perhaps enough has been said to indicate that many novels are concerned with the way in which individual actions achieve, or fail to achieve significance, and that many novels end when a central character has achieved the ability to act significantly, having overcome either his inactivity or his insignificance.

This point, which does have a certain self-evidence about it, does nevertheless have important implications for our general understanding of novels, and as was said above, our general understanding of novels influences the way in which we read particular novels. The present argument, for instance, is intended to negate the claim that novels, especially the so-called 'closed' or traditional, or Victorian, novels end only when the erring character, who has for some reason been living beyond the sanctions of his society, learns to accept his place in it.[8] Characteristic of this point of view is Tony Tanner's comment in his introduction to the Penguin edition of *Mansfield Park*, where he says that in all novels 'we are watching the initially undefined and uncommitted self having to take on definition through what happens to it in society.' To say in contradiction to this that what we watch in fact is the way in which a self *achieves* definition is an apparently minor qualification with major consequences. Two things need to be noticed about Tanner's comment. First, it assumes the passivity of the 'self'. The initial self in the novel is a blank waiting to receive definition—the metaphor he uses is 'take on', which suggests 'put on' as if definition were a suit of clothes applied externally in order to complete the self. Second, society itself is a kind of language, and the individual, the *tabula rasa*, has meaning written on him (or into him) by this language-society. Another way of putting this would be to say that the individual is like a single word that finds meaning only when it finds a place in a sentence; it is the syntax of society that gives the individual word-life meaning, or significance. The individual acquires definition by 'internalising' it (or ingesting it) as the social psychologist would put it. The case is more extreme than even that, however, since the 'self' is forced to eat whether it will or no; meaning is forced down its throat.

As will be seen, these assumptions are directly contrary to the spirit of the major novels to be considered below, in which it can be seen that the self which is to be significantly active in the world is the one that actively projects meaning out there into the hollow potentiality of the forms of language, or society, and by means of this interaction of subjectivity with objectivity *achieves* definition. Novels go to great lengths to make the point of the Romantic poets, that the individual, internal life is the one thing that is *meaningful*. Novels also assert that it is society that has *significance*; it is society that has a system of signs after all. The action of the novel follows the process by means of which that meaning moves towards significance, or embodiment in signs. Both language and society—and society, we have seen, can be regarded as a kind of language—can be represented by a metaphor of clothing, as the phrases 'language is clothing for thought' and 'robes of office, or state' show. Of central importance to the writers of novels is the relationship of the self to these sets of clothing: language and society. Obviously, one cannot do without such clothing, but equally clothes do not make the man. As the saying goes about the sabbath, clothes were made for man and not man for the clothes. When the self is assumed to be passive, clothing begins to take on a life of its own, as in the poem by Elder Olson about M. Chameau who is 'much too fond of fine array' and finds one day that his clothes go out without him. M. Chameau

> Swore not uttering *Sacrebleu*
> Nor *Sacre Nom* nor *Nom de Dieu*
> But rather many and many a *mot*
> *Francais* that you will never know)
> This fantasy of clothes although
> Empty quite of one Chameau
> Strolled most elegantly away
> Through the door and down the stair
> And out upon the pavement where
> The neighbors soon were heard to say
> '*Bonjour, monsieur*' '*Chameau mon cher*
> But you surpass yourself today.'[9]

When clothing is used for array and the self loses sight of the main purpose of clothing, metaphorically speaking, which is the mediation and presentation of self, of interiority, in a public world, then what is merely public takes on a potentially dangerous life of its own. The self that exists only because of its clothing ends up being devoured by the clothing, and the image of the hollow clothes is a universal one it would seem. Without the active infusion of subjective meaning into the signs, or clothes, from the inside, the very forms which make human life possible become cannibalistic and, like the shirt of Nessus, burn their way inwards, devouring subjectivity. Metaphors of clothing and cannibalism seem to belong together and often are used together in fiction. The reason for this is not too difficult to find. Clothing that has a life of its own, is hollow; it is mere form without content, or it is sign without sense, or to use more recent terminology it is a signifier without a signified. It is mere appearance without reality. Now, this hollowness, which is mere objectivity, is a vacuum requiring to be filled; it is hungry. Therefore it devours subjectivity. If we can extrapolate the comic case of M. Chameau into seriousness, once the clothing has devoured the subjectivity of Chameau and used that energy to continue its own superficial life, it begins to be in need of further sustenance and seeks out the subjectivity of others to feed on. When everything vital is transformed into 'surface', the process of devouring is endless. This pattern is central to Dickens; for instance, one need think only of Tulkinghorn and Vholes of *Bleak House*. One small example from Eliot might make the point clearer. Bulstrode, the hypocritical and powerful fundamentalist of *Middlemarch*, is defined by a dogmatic morality, with which his inner self is not fully coincident. He has so fitted himself into a particular mould that the substance of his identity has disappeared. Like all such insubstantial characters, Bulstrode is eventually exposed. The narrator's comment on Bulstrode is: 'There is no general doctrine which is not capable of *eating out our morality* if unchecked by the deep-seated habit of direct fellow-feeling with individual fellow-men.'[10]

Fixed forms, which no longer have any inner life, are a central source of evil in the novel. As the Victorian novelists so clearly saw, what is required to defeat this evil is not a mechanical tinkering with the fixed forms by means of laws or *parliamentary* acts (there is a pun here on 'speech' acts that Dickens didn't miss), but a change of heart in the individual. He must once again begin actively to project meaning—and 'meaning' here means subjectivity or 'fellow feeling' or 'love'—into the inert forms. Not only does this activity of the subject prevent the forms from taking on a destructive life of their own, it also keeps the self from lapsing into solipsism. By putting motive, or intent, to the test by enacting it on a public ground (or in a public medium), the individual imagination protects itself against the narcissistic danger of drowning in itself. If clothing without content can be cannibalistic of subjectivity, then sans-culottism turns out to be another form of cannibalism—it is self-devouring. Again, the logic of this is not hard to follow. In the absence of fixed external forms on which subjectivity can act, the mind must be the inventor of its own forms. And once one set of forms has been invented they begin to take on an independent existence and the process goes on as described above. The archetype of this situation is that of the child warned by its parent not to pull faces lest the wind change and make the face permanent. Having no clothes (or face) at all then is as bad as having nothing but clothes (or faces).

One implication of what has been said is that evil when it appears in fiction will appear as merely a suit of clothes, and when the suit of clothes is attacked by someone, anyone, it will crumble because it has no substance—although it has an apparent significance. Because of the insubstantiality of evil in fiction, many readers have been led to conclude that the novel cannot deal in the categories of Good and Evil, being limited to the merely 'social' categories of right and wrong. Hence Graham Greene's attempt to restore significance to fiction by introducing religious themes and making damnation—self-damnation as Scobie of *The Heart of the Matter* believes—possible in novels. Greene's solution is not convincing, however, and it is not convincing because it is a solution to a problem that does not really exist. The mistake is to assume that the 'suit of clothes' personality, the personality who manipulates surface signs without sincerity, without really being there, is guilty of a merely social fault. The novel testifies that the misuse of the signs of human community is a metaphysical evil; it condemns one to a lack of substance. It is not necessary for evil to be melodramatic; it need not be measured by the number of effects it produces. Evil, that is to say, cannot be considered quantitatively since what is at stake is quality—the quality of being, of identity, of ultimate reality of the human personality. As Yeats has it, in 'Lapis Lazuli', apocalypse is an absolute:

> Though Hamlet rambles and Lear rages,
> And all the drop-scenes drop at once
> Upon a hundred thousand stages,
> It cannot grow by an inch or an ounce.

Characters afflicted with the evil of insubstantiality are certainly productive of evil in the life of their communities and to the extent that they lead others to imitate their insubstantiality they are productive of absolute evil, qualitatively. What the novelist sees, however, is that evil is its own worst enemy; insubstantiality is self-defeating. If evil takes the form of the hollow word, or the hollow clothes of a mechanical society, then obviously what is required is a change of heart on the part of the individual member of that society. Evil is after all a metaphysical notion. When it appears, however, it appears in merely social categories: that is, the evil man is the one who is merely 'social' and has no 'soul'. To argue that a metaphysical evil, signalled by a social phenomenon, should be cured by tinkering with the social mechanism, is an absurdity that the Victorian novelists were conscious of. Hence the idiocy of the comment (not so often heard nowadays) that although Dickens could analyse social ills he could offer no solution. He offered exactly the solution appropriate to his analysis of the situation. What is wanting is spirit and that cannot be legislated externally; it must arise from within.

Another charge one often hears against the novel is that it is too optimistic; it cannot really describe the evils of life because writing itself is a positive creative activity, and therefore absolute negativity is an impossibility for the novel. And therefore the novel with its happy ending is a bourgeois genre, pandering to middle-class need for comfort and reassurance. The matter can be put differently. Because a novel ends 'happily' is not necessarily evidence that the author has failed to face real problems of evil, or negativity. In Dickens, as we shall see, the problems he set himself are ones that are perhaps never soluble. The world appears often to be all a muddle, with no possibility of an ordered and happy life. What a novelist like Dickens often does is to present his perception of the logical impossibility of existence with meticulous and almost insane care—and then ignore the fact that life seems logically impossible. This logical inconsistency is the stuff of fiction, where magic occurs, and the positive vision that emerges from a vision of evil is a novelist's expression of faith, which has no logic or necessity. In fact, it is part of the happy joke of fiction that it, in itself, is the solution to the evils it describes, since fiction, fantasy, imagination is precisely the thing that stimulates the inner growth that needs to be projected out into the mechanical forms of society and language to keep life possible. It is not surprising, according to the modified structural argument being pursued in this chapter, that the novelist should present evil in such a way as to echo his own preoccupations as a writer. Evil is insignificance—the one thing a writer of fiction needs most to fear. The other form of evil, and it is the same thing under a different form, is significance that has taken on a life of its own—significance which is not intended, or is hypocritically intended and is therefore bad or false art. Now, the writer who uses language for telling a story faces the benign danger of having the story take over. He must know exactly at what point to pursue actively his own designs and at what point to become passive and let the story have its way with him. It is out of such active–passivity that stories grow. Further, he is using language for fiction, to tell lies. And he does this because he is trying to infuse new meaning into the surface significance of life. He wants us to look below the surface, and he must manipulate the surface in such a way to make us do this. If he fails in his craft, we will see the surface delights only and dismiss him as possibly significant, but ultimately meaningless. If he fails at a deeper level, in the depths of his sincerity, of his caring, there will be no meaning there for us to find, and likely little significance either. For the writer having to use public signs to convey a private meaning, and having to lie in order to succeed in telling the truth, it is not surprising at all that his own preoccupations should reappear as structural elements in his work.

One final word about the insubstantiality of evil and the evil of insubstantiality. It is perhaps true after all that the novel does not altogether face the character who is absolutely evil, who is an embodied negation of everything, whatever form that sort of character could take. Perhaps Blandois of *Little Dorrit*, who has absolutely no respect for the forms of language or society, is as close as one can come, and he too remains an insubstantial figure. Novels present evil by means of words, and words are a kind of clothing, which can mislead and can become cannabilistic. Now, the figure of absolute evil is the one who is hollow in his heart, who is void within. He is cannibalistic and destructive. When this cannibal appears in words, however, he is in danger of devouring himself and the very mechanical forms of society which are often the weapons of his evil-doing turn out also to be the forms of civilisation which work towards the preservation of human life. The clothes of civilisation may be cannibalistic then, but it is also one of the lovely ironies of fiction, and life, that when the cannibal is clothed, or civilised, his capacity for evil is by that much diminished. This point will be developed in the next chapter with reference to the archetypal linguistic cannibal, Caliban.

The purpose of his chapter has been to define a set of terms by using them. The rest of the book will be devoted to discussing individual texts in the hope that the meanings that emerge there will continue to give the terms value. Briefly once again, the cluster of terms arises as follows. Man is an agent and he acts in and by signs; his action is mediated. From that arises the possibility of hypocrisy: of wearing words and clothes without meaning what they signify in appearance. The novelist's persona is a particularly acute form of this hypocrisy since he must use the apparent significances of words to mean something quite different from what they do in fact mean. His is a benign hypocrisy and he is at pains to distinguish benign from evil hypocrisy. Hypocrisy is a form of drama and the novel is therefore structurally committed to the attempt to differentiate benign from evil drama. The origin of the interest in drama is the personal confrontation of 'my meaning' with the 'world's meaning'. When there is no 'speaker's meaning' the words become mere clothing, as does the person who merely puts on the suit of clothes offered him by society; the clothes take on a life of their own and become cannibalistic of human subjectivity. This cannibalism arises from insubstantiality and is itself seen to be insubstantial. The reason for this insubstantiality lies at least in part in the fact that while the clothes may be cannibalistic, the cannibal clothed is less dangerous than an absolute negativity that denies the validity of all forms and significances in the world.

2 From Shakespeare to Congreve: Between Drama and Novel

The way in which *The Tempest* deals with the question of who ought to rule, or who ought to wear the robes of state and how, might well seem to some to be completely arbitrary. Prospero's historical claim to the title of Duke of Milan might be thought to be equivalent to Caliban's historical claim to be the ruler of his island. In order to oust the usurping Duke, his brother, Prospero must usurp the rule of Caliban, and the conclusion that one might be tempted to draw is that the play is a poetic exercise in dressing to advantage the Machiavellian message that it is after all the powerful that will rule. Whatever suggestive value such comments have, the play itself does not seem to lead us towards a relativity on the question of who ought to rule. The opening scene is implicitly one about authority, and the authority in question is one that is not necessarily to be identified with position, or role. The Boatswain, as the ship is about to crack in the tempest conjured up by Prospero, has no time for the presumptions of rank and complains that the noise made by the cries of the royal and noble passengers 'is louder than the weather, or our office'. In a situation of extremity, 'office' becomes what it really is: not a position abstractly or historically defined, but simply the action appropriate to the situation at hand. Office, that is to say, is nothing but significant action. The cries and protests of Alonso, Sebastian *et al.* do not work towards saving the ship, and their rank or role is useless. When they attempt to exercise their 'authority', they are rebuked by the Boatswain who says to Gonzalo:

> You are a counsellor: if you can command these elements to silence, and work the peace of the present, we will not hand a rope more; use your authority: if you cannot, give thanks you have lived so long, and make yourself ready in your cabin for the mischance of the hour. . . .

The Boatswain's speech points to the absurd limits of all worldly or merely social authority: it cannot command the elements, nor death. We are reminded, however, that there is one, Prospero, who has had enough authority to command the elements, since it is he who has conjured up the tempest. Obviously, in practical terms, the authority of Prospero to do the impossible cannot be compared with the more mundane authority of kings and princes. The argument of the play is not that Prospero ought to be restored to temporal rule because he has magical power over the elements. The fantasy world of the play, and the magical power that Prospero has achieved, point to the fact that the play is not a political treatise. And yet it is about real authority; which is to say that the poetic, or magical aspects of the play are to have our first attention, and that these aspects may then be seen to have political implications.

Unlike the other characters, Prospero's activity is not quite so limited by his situation. As an actor he is able to do away with some of the passivity with respect to the 'stage' of action that is usually necessary. He can command the stage to do what he wills and since he can create the ground for whatever action he requires, he can do what he likes merely by producing the appropriate setting. In terms of the 'scene-agent' ratio, the agent is dominant. This means that there must be some qualitative difference in the agent. This turns out to be the case as Prospero's early explanation to Miranda makes clear. As he begins to explain to his daughter the details of his history, he removes his robe, asking Miranda for help to 'pluck my magic garment from me'. He then says, putting the robe down, 'Lie there, my art.' His magic is a kind of garment, which can be put on and off, as it will turn out that robes of state are clothes which can once again fittingly be put on at the end of the play. Indeed, the action moves from the doffing of one set of clothes towards the donning of another. The magic of the play is designed to make clear to the usurpers that they are unsuitable wearers of the robes of state. Prospero has attained the ability to wear magic robes partly as a result of his showing his unsuitableness as a young man for the robes of state. As Prospero explains to Miranda, his brother, Antonio:

> he whom next thyself
> Of all the world I lov'd, and to him put
> The manage of my state, as at that time
> Through all the signories it was the first,
> And Prospero the prime duke, being so reputed
> In dignity, and for the liberal arts
> Without a parallel; those being all my study,
> The government I cast upon my brother
> And to my state grew stranger, being transported
> And rapt in secret studies . . .

Prospero becomes inactive by becoming a stranger to his 'state' and casts the robes of office upon his brother. The result of this is that Antonio begins to cover his brother as a kind of parasitical garment so that

> now he was
> The ivy which had hid my princely trunk
> And *suck'd my verdure out on't.*
>
> [my italics]

The clothes of state, when inappropriately worn, or hollow, become cannibalistic of the essence of the one who should be wearing them. But Prospero really earns his right to the robes of office by giving them up. His secret studies are essential here. He descends inside himself and develops that full internality that makes it possible for one to wear clothes without falling into the conflict between personal identity and role. Prospero's secret studies lead him to develop that magical internal property, which is like the source of poetry, or the power to weave 'spells'.

The ability to wear the tricky clothes of either poetry or state derives from the initial development of the inner man. In order to be a public agent, one must first have been passive in secret. It is only the patient who can become a fully effective and powerful agent. The beginning of the play shows us in the powerful, authoritative Prospero the end result of such a process of personal growth. The pattern of his life is the pattern that literature again and again urges us towards. The first requirement is a plunge into the depths, followed by a re-emergence into 'clothing'. At that stage one can begin to cut the clothes to the required fit. One should also note Prospero's short-tempered rebukes to the supposedly inattentive Miranda as an instance of what might happen to the personality that does not come back from the magic world of dreams to the public world of 'reality'. Prospero himself is at the crisis point of his life, and must now surrender his power completely to work his will by manipulating the scene, and submit his agency to the passivity of wearing the robes of state. The public clothes provide him a medium for his agency, and this medium will keep him human. Left alone on the island with his private magic, we might imagine him turning into a version of his predecessor, Sycorax. Prospero must set Ariel free in order to become mere man once again and by so doing keep himself from becoming less than human.

In the play, of course, Prospero is in motion towards re-appearance in society. He is ready to resume his customary robes and the magic of the play works to purify the clothing of the wrongfully established rulers, as Gonzalo's comment on their 'drowning' indicates:

> our garments, being, as they were drench'd in the sea, hold, notwithstanding, their freshness and glosses, being rather new-dy'd than stain'd with salt water.

This echoes what Ariel has already told Prospero: 'On their sustaining garments not a blemish,/ But fresher than before . . . .' The sea-change of Alonso *et al.* is an echo of the immersion of Prospero in his own depths and the re-emergence of those who are themselves newly 'died' is signalled by the dyeing into newness of their clothing. The pun on dyeing is part of the universal upside-downness of the world of the play. Just as one must die in order to live, so too it was necessary for Prospero to take off the robes of state as a youth in order, later to be fit to wear them. The converse situation is demonstrated by Antonio and Sebastian. Antonio counsels Sebastian to murder Alonso and become ruler in his stead. When Sebastian appears totally ignorant of the motive that Antonio would like to see active in him, Antonio says:

> If you but knew how you the purpose cherish
> Whiles thus you mock it! how, in stripping it,
> You more invest it!

The inverse logic of Antonio's hortatory rhetoric suggests that, while Sebastian appears to be taking off the garment of ambition, he is in fact the more putting it on. The hint of the metaphor is also intended, that Sebastian, while he pretends not to desire the robes of rule worn by his brother, 'really' signals, to those who can read, the intensity with which he desires them. These treasonable plotters reverse logic for purposes of evil. They mock the logic of the goodly Gonzalo when he has a vision of rule that seems logically impossible:

> I' th' commonwealth I would by contraries
> Execute all things; for no kind of traffic
> Would I admit; no name of magistrate;
> Letters should not be known; riches, poverty,
> And use of service, none; contract, succession,
> Bourn, bound of land, tilth, vineyard, none;
> No use of metal, corn, or wine, or oil;
> No occupation; all men idle, all;
> And women too, but innocent and pure;
> No sovereignty.

To which Sebastian replies, 'Yet he would be king on't', an apparently crushing rejoinder. And yet the rule described by Gonzalo just falls short of the rule that Prospero himself is working towards. Gonzalo envisions the naturalness of artificial rule; he seems to see rule without sovereignty. His vision is a hollow one because he lacks the essential authority to enact it; it is therefore deserving of the mockery of Antonio and Sebastian, even if not deserving complete dismissal. Prospero is the one, it is suggested, who can achieve that state where 'office' no longer will destroy the man (the 'role' will be natural), and similarly where the office will be safe from the plotting man. Prospero, having undergone the preparation of the internal sea-change, can re-emerge and accomplish the paradoxical unification of office and individual because he has learned how to wear the clothes of office; both how actively to wear them so as not to be merely a suit of clothes, and how passively to wear them so that individual self-seeking does not destroy or 'stain' the clothes.

Stephano and Trinculo reveal the comic stupidity of those who believe that mere clothing is the source of authority. Urged on by Caliban, they set off to kill Prospero and take over the island for themselves. Ariel, at Prospero's bidding, had decked a 'line' tree with gaudy clothing, which proves the perfect ruse for the would-be assassins. Caliban is much shrewder, and dismisses the clothing with, 'Let it alone, thou fool! It is but trash.' The important thing is 'to do the murder first'. Caliban's earlier advice had been, 'First to possess his books', and 'Burn but his books.' He misses the point, however, for just as clothes are mere trappings or trash, and what is important is who wears them and how, so too mere language as contained in books is not the source of Prospero's strength. The secret communion he has had with them is. Caliban's later motive, 'do the murder first', is therefore a more practical one since it is Prospero, in himself, who stands in the way and merely possessing his external attributes, his clothing or his books, will not put him in their power.

Now, the relative depth of insight of Caliban on these two points is noteworthy for another reason. He shows himself to have some perception of the lack of worth of mere 'clothing', but he does not show a full understanding of authority, or language, or books. Caliban has had the pleasure of being taught language by Miranda, but he remains incapable of the higher reaches of development that language makes available. Miranda rebukes him thus:

> Abhorred slave,
> Which any print of goodness wilt not take,
> Being capable of all ill! I pitied thee,
> Took pains to make thee speak, taught thee each hour
> One thing or other. When thou didst not, savage,
> Know thine own meaning, but wouldst gabble like
> A thing most brutish, I endow'd thy purposes
> With words that made them known. But thy vile race,
> Though thou didst learn, had that in't which good natures
> Could not abide to be with. Therefore wast thou
> Deservedly confin'd into this rock, who hadst
> Deserv'd more than a prison.

The central point of this seems to be that while Caliban can take the imprint of language ('thou didst learn') he is incapable of receiving 'any print of goodness'. He is, as Prospero says, 'a born devil, on whose nature/Nurture can never stick!' Although Caliban, then, can be clothed in language, the clothing cannot be made to stick and, further, he lacks that inner nature that would allow him adequately to wear the clothes of human being. Caliban's response to Miranda, of course, is to say:

> You taught me language, and my profit on't
> Is, I know how to curse. The red plague rid you
> For learning me your language!

Caliban (whose name we know Shakespeare derived from a newly popular word 'cannibal') has not the inner nature that will allow him to make the external trappings of language—the merely significant—into meaningful utterances, or into poetry, or the language of love. Language has, according to Miranda's speech, made his own meaning evident to him, and this knowledge leads him to curse.

Caliban never has, and never develops, that mysterious inner nature that really gives one power in language, but continues to treat it as something merely external, like clothing. Hence his mistaken belief that power over Prospero can be had by burning his language. In the scenes with Stephano and Trinculo, Shakespeare gives further indications of the 'externality' of Caliban's relation to language. Stephano, offering him the bottle, says 'Come on your ways. Open your mouth. Here is that which will give language to you, cat. Open your mouth.' Stephano is a parodic version of Gonzalo who addresses Alonso and is rewarded with the comment: 'You cram these words into mine ears against the stomach of my sense.' Even if he were to eat the words of sense that are being crammed into him, Alonso could not benefit from them, since, significant though they may be, he is inwardly blind to their meaning. So too Caliban ingests language like drink, or drink like language, but it does not produce the desired results. Inspiration must come from within; it is self-born and cannot be ingested. The result of Caliban's attempt to swallow language is that the 'man-monster hath drowned his tongue in sack'. Unlike the monstrous men who undergo a sea change and as a result of this internal drowning emerge able to wear new-dyed clothes again, it is only Caliban's tongue, mere flesh, that is drowned.

One must conclude that any attempt to treat the play in merely political terms or to argue that the play presents a power struggle in which the strongest, Prospero, wins out over the weakest, is to misread; or it is to be guilty of reading merely the surface signals without attention to their meaning. Caliban deserves prison, as Miranda suggests. But prison is not enough for him, because a prison is a social or political instrument and Caliban's offences, in their proper order of magnitude, are first against nature, then language, and then against the order of society. The last of those offences is not in any way the original one; it is rather the necessary corollary of the others. Caliban's curses are a testimony to the fact that the degree to which he has learned language is the degree also to which he has lost his ability merely to work evil. He is a hybrid now, a 'man-monster', and not merely 'monster'. Although language might be thought to have eaten out the evil resolve, or power of Caliban, from another point of view, the cannibal (Caliban) clothed is already on his way to being civilised, to being human. Clothing itself can be cannabilistic of essence, as the examples of Alonso and Sebastian show. Prospero rediscovers essence and then puts on the clothes, as is proper. Caliban has a cannibalistic nature and for such a one in whom 'nature' is unremittingly evil, the potentially cannibal clothes serve a desirable function. At least the cannibal is clothed.

What I hope this analysis of a single play by Shakespeare will reveal is not that there is a fixed pattern of meaning and image that novelists take over from him and use consistently throughout the growth of that genre. Instead, I would like to see Shakespeare as providing in compressed essence some of the topics that will be seen naturally to recur in other writers. By this I mean to suggest that when similar dramatic and linguistic and clothing topics turn up, they do so not merely as a result of the influence of the bard, but rather because they must do so when a writer attempts to structure his meaning in signs. *The Tempest* turns on a discontinuity between self and social role, and in the case of Miranda and Ferdinand between desire and duty, which is resolved by fantasy, magic, poetry. There is an awareness of a gap that must exist between the inner man and the outer world. Prospero's example suggests that with spiritual effort a man can learn to bridge this gap and live in the world, and if he does then he serves as a sufficient catalyst to make the rest of the world begin to be a possible place. Now, obviously this solution by 'romance' would not be acceptable to the novel, which, as we know, begins by reacting against the excessive romance of previous times, as in *Don Quixote*. As I hope to show in a minute, there is a discontinuity with the romantic aspects of *The Tempest* in the beginnings of the novel, but there is also a striking continuity. The novel cuts away the solution by romance, or fantasy, in favour of greater plausibility or reality, but it does not abandon certain dramatic elements. This means that the ideal offered by *The Tempest* remains as a never quite realised goal; an ideal which reality (the mode of the novel) must always just fail to reach but continue to strive for. The same dramatic matrix recurs: that of subjectivity striving to realise itself by 'filling' hollow forms (or clothes). What disappears is the confidence that there can be a full coincidence of inner and outer, or love and duty, or self and social role, or meaning and significance (signifier-signified). In terms of the history of literature one can, by taking a very rough view of the matter, suggest that the novel arises not because the middle classes arise, but rather because the drama declines. With minor exceptions the story of the theatre after Shakespeare is that of the decadence of the drama and the emergence of the novel as the central genre of our culture, as it continues to be. One can link this fact—as Ian Watt does in his discussion of individualism in *The Rise of the Novel*—with the development of excessive innerness as a result of the Puritan revolution and the second turn of the screw of subjectivity in the Romantic movement. As subjectivity becomes more intense, the gap between self and the world, or between self and word, increases. Drama, that most public and social of genres, becomes more difficult to produce, even though it remains as an ideal. The Romantic poets themselves epitomise the problem: striving to write dramas and producing that unactable thing, a 'closet drama'. The novel finds its dramatic focus by keeping two dynamic poles in opposition: that of the subjective self and that of the fixed forms of society. What results is not the re-appearance of a single structural pattern, but an infinitely varied series of stories which can more or less be seen to centre around the topics we have delimited, taking now one pole to be dominant, now another.

We must back up briefly to the Elizabethan world once again, in order to take advantage of some ideas from a very important book: *Idea and Act in Elizabethan Fiction* by Walter R. Davis (Princeton, N.J., 1969). Davis discusses Sydney's defence of fictions and considers certain elements of theatre in the world of Elizabethan fiction. One thing that makes fictions acceptable is that they present the ideal as if it were actuality; or rather that they show ideals embodied in action and therefore present the ideal as possibility and therefore fiction 'can be an act of speculation, an excursion into the realm of what is possible in human existence'.[1] Davis argues, most convincingly, that, given their focus on the ideal and the actual, the Elizabethans also focused on language as mediator—note that one could present this argument in reverse form: because they were interested in language, they were interested in the relationship of ideal, or possible, to actual:

> If the end of fiction as the Elizabethans conceived it was to discover the area of contact between the ideal and the actual in life, then one of the most important means by which such a 'fore-conceit' issued into actual narrative was a peculiarly strong sense of role-playing. For whatever causes . . . we find common to much Elizabethan poetry and prose the sense that to write is essentially to speak, to speak is essentially to act out a part.[2]

Here is another way of stating what was argued in the previous chapter: that it is the individual confrontation of self and language that gives rise to the dramatic elements of literature. Davis goes on to argue that the 'play-acting' is acceptable because it is the only means of enacting an ideal. Implicit in this of course is the suggestion that play-acting that does not enact an ideal, hollow play-acting, will be unacceptable. He believes that what happens between the end of Elizabethan fiction and the emergence of the novel is the disappearance of the ideal. Although he does not make the point, his argument is exactly the one needed to account for the fact that as soon as the novel begins, it shows an uncommon interest in the figure of the hypocrite: the play-actor who is not enacting an ideal. One reason for returning to Davis is that he mentions *The Tempest*:

It is because they touch ideals that these histrionics become significant.
. . . But the role must be given up at the end of the play, for while it
extends the possibilities of action for the hero it also cramps his normally
various personality into the strict and narrow channel of purpose. The
role distorts to tell the truth or accomplish the purpose, and hence the
hero hastens towards the point where it can be destroyed. The tragic
mode merges the role and the full self at the hero's death, as in Othello's
last act; the comic insists on a ritual undressing, of which Prospero's
return to common humanity is a striking example.[3]

If we substitute, as a larger category, our term 'clothing' where Davis uses
role, it can be seen that his remarks are appropriate. One might, however,
make one or two minor qualifications. One could, for instance, argue that in
tragedy we see the complete divergence of individual and role, so that
Othello's death occurs when his occupation is gone and he sacrifices all
matters of state for a private passion. One could say the same of Lear, who
divides his kingdom on a private whim. And Lear ends with what could
perhaps be called a ritual undressing: 'Pray you, undo this button.' Of
comedy, Davis seems closer to the mark when he speaks of the distance that
comedy reveals between self and role. And yet we have already seen that
Prospero does not 'undress', he changes dress and the play concludes with
the resumption (metaphorically) of the robes of office. *The Tempest*, by
making the redressing a ritual one, or one that needs consciously to be
undertaken, stresses the proper relationship that ought to hold between
clothing (of office or of language) and self. There must be a formal distance
but not a radical distinction. This qualification allows us now to move on to
a final passage from Davis, which contains a name a little surprising,
perhaps, to students of the novel:

> It is a curious but undeniable fact that fiction of distinction all but dis-
> appears between the death of Elizabeth and the accession of Charles II,
> and it is the province of a different kind of study from ours to trace the
> process, causes and effects of the decline. When original fiction arose in
> England again in Bunyan and Congreve, and later in Defoe and
> Richardson, it appeared rewoven on the loom of history, of probable fact,
> as Congreve affirmed. But it was a new kind of history, not so much that
> of man facing other men, much less nature or concepts, as of man facing
> himself, the internal history of the mind as conveyed first by such sub-
> literary genres as the Puritan diary or spiritual autobiography. William
> Congreve and his contemporaries thought of the novel as a complete
> departure from earlier fiction, bearing little relation to it other than that of
> burlesque to its target; we have every reason to accept their judgment in
> the matter.[4]

Congreve, one might ask? What on earth is he doing in there? Davis's hint is worth following up, however, although what one finds in Congreve's novella, *Incognita* (1713), does not exactly bear out what Davis asserts. True enough, in his 'Preface to the Reader', Congreve is highly critical of 'romances', 'where lofty language, miraculous contingencies and impossible performances, elevate and surprize the reader into a giddy delight, which leaves him flat upon the ground whenever he leaves of[f] . . . '. He contrasts with the implausible romances of knights the more acceptable novel:

> Novels are of a more familiar nature; come near us . . . delight us with accidents and odd events, but not such as are wholly unusual or unpresidented, such which not being so distant from our belief bring also the pleasure nearer us. Romances give us more of wonder, novels more delight.

As it turns out, *Incognita* is neither romance nor novel. It is a parody of romance; its intrigues are highly contrived and the whole thing is an ironic explosion of the romance tradition. It does not offer us events that come near us, but rather gives us a romance which deliberately leaves us flat upon the ground because of its ironic suggestion that such a working out of events is impossible. Briefly, Aurelian and his friend Hippolito arrive incognito in Florence, Aurelian's home city, where it is expected he will complete a marriage contract made in infancy between himself and one Juliana. By means of disguises, the two young men attend a ball and are smitten by two fair maids: Hippolito by Leonora, although he gives his name as Aurelian; Aurelian by an unknown who calls herself Incognita, while Aurelian tells her that his name is Hippolito. Predictable confusion arises; there is a melodramatic murder in a cathedral and so on. The subtitle of the novella is *Love and Duty Reconcil'd*. Incognita, it turns out, is Juliana, who knows she has soon to marry the expected Aurelian; she has of course fallen in love with 'Hippolito', who is really Aurelian under a false name. When she is about to follow her inclinations and satisfy Love at the expense of Duty, the mysteries are cleared up and everything ends happily.

Clearly the story line is little different from stock romance plots. One suspects also that there is a continuity between Elizabethan plots and Congreve, despite Davis's disclaimer. What makes *Incognita* striking is the narrative tone, which is one of crippling irony, suggesting at times that the narrator just cannot be bothered to go on with such nonsense. When he tries to express what Aurelian felt upon first seeing the face of Incognita, he instead explains why this is impossible: 'In short, to be made sensible of his condition, we must conceive some idea of what he beheld, which is not to be imagined till seen, nor then to be express'd.' This, by the way, would be true of novels as well as of parodic romance. A description does follow, but it is deliberately non-functional and presented in the tritest of dress. Painters are vaguely referred to, as is Venus. Eyes diffuse warm rays that could melt frozen hearts; the rays are said to be of such power that they could enter through the pores. She is majestic, affable, and alluring. Of the whole experience it is said that 'none but lovers who have experience of such visions will believe'. Here we come upon a radical discontinuity between internal and external; what is felt cannot be expressed and what is expressed is inadequate to create a sense of that internality.

This theme has been suggested in an earlier discussion between Aurelian and Incognita on clothing, Aurelian contending that '"probable conjectures may be made of the ingenious disposition of the mind, from the fancy and choice of apparel"'. Incognita counters with the comment,

'tis possible a fool may reveal himself by his dress, in wearing something extravagantly singular and ridiculous, or in preposterous suiting of colours; but a decency of habit (which is all that men of best sense pretend to) may be acquired by custom and example, without putting the person to a superfluous expence of wit for the contrivance.

This carries the day. The point is that clothing and language are both 'general' things, not suited to the accurate presentation of particulars of individual character. We may get some clue from the external clothing, indeed we have no other choice but to assume that the signals are meaningful, until we can interpret them, or see beyond them. The narrative irony begins to suggest that the coincidence of inner and outer, or Love and Duty, is not such an easy matter as romances suggest.

As this parodic romance approaches a satisfactory conclusion, instances of irony become more common. The 'content' of the story is repeatedly asserted to be so much better than what is presented to the reader. Aurelian by means of a fine speech, gets himself out of a contretemps: the 'excuse was so handsomly designed, and much better express'd than it is here, that it took effect'. Shortly Aurelian makes another 'very passionate and eloquent speech in behalf of himself (much better than I intend to insert here) and expressed a mighty concern . . . '. Incognita has been telling Aurelian of her plight, but the narrator cautions us: '"For I would caution the reader by the bye, not to believe every word which she told him, nor that admirable sorrow which she counterfeited to be accurately true. It was indeed truth so cunningly intermingled with fiction . . ."'. Of Aurelian's love 'rhetorick' we learn, ''Twere tedious to tell the many ingenious arguments he used . . .'. Enough has been said, perhaps, to demonstrate that the tired, ironic contempt of the tone of the telling completely undercuts the tale. The story works to the reconciliation of love and duty, but the telling of it convinces one that such reconcilation takes place only in fiction. In real life there is a crucial gap between inclination and necessity, and it is only by artful

'contrivance', a word that occurs frequently in *Incognita*, that such reconcilation comes about. In his Preface, to which we must now return, Congreve points to the contrivance of the tale when he comments on the
relation the 'unity' of his tale has to the classical 'unities': 'In a comedy this
would be called the unity of action; here it may pretend to no more than an
unity of contrivance.'

Now, it is with the Preface that we can come back to the main point: is
there any continuity with Elizabethan literature in Congreve's tale—which,
it is necessary to repeat, is more a parodic romance that it is a novel?
Congreve very carefully distinguishes the terms romance, novel, comedy,
tragedy, and drama. He says that 'the drama is the long extracted from
romance and history: 'tis the mid-wife to industry, and brings forth alive the
conceptions of the brain'. The gap between inner and outer, between
imagination and expression that cripples the romance of *Incognita* is overcome in one medium: 'the mid-wife' drama. *Incognita* itself, we might
suspect, is intended to be a dramatic exposure of romance. It will not lecture
us on the inadequacies of romance; it will instead enact the absurdities
before our eyes and it will be, as the narrator suggests, 'the dullest reader in
the world' who does not get the message. Congreve goes quite far in his
praise of the drama:

> Since all traditions must indisputably give place to the drama, and since
> there is no possibility of giving that life to the writing or repetition of a
> story which it has in the action, I resolved in another beauty to imitate
> dramatick writing, namely, in the design, contexture and result of the
> plot. I have not observed it before in a novel . . . . If there be any thing
> more in particular resembling the copy which I imitate (as the curious
> reader will soon perceive) I leave it to show it self, being very well
> satisfy'd how much more proper it had been for him to have found out
> this himself.

This neglected critical comment on the novel is perhaps one of the most
important we have, coming as it does right at the birth of the genre. It makes
absolutely clear the connection the novel will have with Elizabethan literature: it will continue to be fascinated with elements of drama. The story
itself turns our attention to the crucial matter of how personal identity can
ever be expressed in the 'clothing' available in the world. It ironically
presents the impossible task of the novel, which must bridge that very gap.
The easy solution by way of romance is thrown out. Congreve does not
solve the problem he sets, but he does provide most of the elements that will
re-appear as the novel continues its 'excursion into the realm of what is
possible in human existence'. Although the total irony of *Incognita* suggests
the impossibility of ever reconciling love and duty, inner and outer, self and
society, the crucial clue is offered in Congreve's emphasis on the dramatic
aspects that the novel takes into its core from the beginning. The story of the

novel from Congreve on is the story of a search for that particular kind of drama, in the novel and in life, that will allow the conceptions of the brain to be brought forth alive, or the idea one has of oneself to become significantly active in the world.

3 The Thread in the Garment

One central meaning of the metaphor of the world as theatre that has not yet been considered, is that the material world is the theatre in which the soul enacts its drama; related to this is the saying that the body is the clothing of the soul which both permits and enforces activity in the temporal, mortal drama. We find this sense of the metaphor occurring in Richardson's *Clarissa*.[1] Near the end of her tribulations, Clarissa prays for submission to God's will and 'doubted not but by the Divine goodness she should be a happy creature as soon as she could be divested of these *rags of mortality*'.[2] Lovelace's adviser, Belford, reminds him that Clarissa is celebrated for beauty '"and so noted at the same time for prudence, for *soul* (I will say, instead of *sense*), and for virtue. . ."'.[3] Again and again the intense internality of Clarissa is stressed; even Lovelace confesses that he recognises this fact, '"She is thou sayest, *all mind*. So say I"'.[4] The story of her torments and ultimate moral victory, is the story of the power of soul, or 'mind', over mere matter. One implication of this is that the novel will show little concern with mediation; the soul is of such virtue that, unlike the later concept which will replace it, self—already hinted at in the parenthetical comment indicating the linguistic rivalry between 'sense' and 'soul'—it does not need to pay attention to methods of presenting itself in everyday life. There may be temporary misunderstandings, or misinterpretations, but the real strength of the inner world will at last shine through, as Miss Howe suggests in repeating a comment of Clarissa's: '"My countenance, said she, is indeed an honest picture of my heart. But the mind will run away with the body at any time."'[5] The issue is not complicated by considerations of symbolic transformation.

This power of mind or soul is operative only when one conducts oneself in such a way as to preserve soul, however. Lovelace, as his name indicates, is a mere lover of the clothing (lace) and ignores the essence. At one point he refuses a companion because he is a fop, '"and a fop . . . takes great pains to hang out a sign by his dress of what he has in his shop"'.[6] Lovelace is blind to the fact that he is himself a moral fop, and that his clothing betrays that his shop is empty. Ultimately he begins to discover that his apparent strength is weakness, and finds himself developing a love for Clarissa that is ' "*less personal*, as I may say, more *intellectual*, than ever I thought it could be to woman"'.[7] Without, perhaps, realising the truth of what he says, Lovelace says to Belford, after Clarissa's death, ' "we don't make ourselves, except it be worse by our dress'''.[8] In apparent repentance, he accurately sums up his life: '"What a cursed still-life was this! Nothing active in me, or about me, but the worm that never dies."'[9] So his apparent activity, and his merely worldly power wither away; and the apparent passivity of Clarissa proves paradoxically to have been the higher form of agency after all.

As in Congreve, there is a radical split between the inner and the outer worlds, and although Richardson does not show the sardonic and ironic scepticism of Congreve, he too seems to suggest that the happy unification of inner self with the demands of the external world occurs only in romance. Richardson, however, shows greater confidence than does Congreve that the essential soul can appear and be known, despite the hypocritical management of public signals by such as Lovelace. For a time Lovelace has it all his own way, and all of Clarissa's family accuse her 'of acting with *deep art*'.[10] Of course, Clarissa is acting with deep heart, and Lovelace with superficial art. Like Congreve, Richardson seems instinctively to have turned to the theatre for the informing essence of his art.[11] Despite the epistolary form, we find the characters often in dramatic exchanges; indeed the letters often recount dramatic encounters and developments. Lovelace himself is, of course, the bad actor, the hypocrite. He himself admits that he is 'not a bad mimic'[12] although he denies that he is a hypocrite. His bad acting arises from the fact that he has no inner source of agency, no character or soul, and therefore he can, 'like the devil in Milton',[13] assume many shapes. Even Clarissa is sometimes confused by him, and calls him a 'perfect Proteus'.

Now, the question is, is Lovelace active and therefore evil, and is Clarissa passive and therefore good? This would be a conclusion that would fit with the claim that Richardson presents theatrical elements in order to show that they are evil. These two conclusions would not, however, be reconcilable with the claim that Richardson's art is itself dramatic. Either that, or one would have to conclude that his art is in conflict with his morality. It turns out, however, that Richardson is engaged in that central task of novels, trying to differentiate between benign and malign drama. It is not altogether true, as it appears to be at first, that Clarissa, because she is the true light, will shine through irrespective of medium. She herself has yielded to Miss Howe's urgings that she record her 'tragical story' in letters, in the hope that it will 'be of as much use as honour to the sex'.[14] Clarissa believes that Mr Belford, 'when he comes to revolve the whole story, placed before him in *one strong light* . . . may so regulate his future actions . . .'.[15] The strong light will shine through, if the art sets out all signals in the proper order. As Lovelace says, '"glossing over *one* part of a story, and *omitting another*, . . . will make a bad cause a good one at any time"'.[16]

The point is, of course, that managing only the surface of signs can only make things worse; it is only when there is inner light that the surface can be sufficiently made to carry a message. Clarissa is ultimately capable of 'significant action' because she works from inner to outer, and because of her *sense* she is capable of greater drama than is Lovelace. Echoing Christ's words, she indulges in a small 'artifice' in a letter to Lovelace, which says in part:

> I am setting out with all diligence for my Father's House. I am bid to hope that he will receive his poor penitent with a goodness peculiar to himself; for I am overjoyed with the assurance of a thorough reconciliation, through the interposition of a dear, blessed friend whom I always loved and honoured.[17]

Clarissa confesses to Mr Belford that this letter was only a stratagem, an artifice, and wonders if it were justified, but then almost archly adds, ' "Yet, 'tis strange too, that neither you nor he found out my meaning on perusal of my letter." '.[18] For those already aware of the 'meaning', the signals are perfectly adequate; for those who do not have the right kind of eyes to see, but focus their attention on the surface only, the signs are hollow. Of course, it takes a particular inability to read, or an exceptional blindness to signs, not to have spotted the significance of the capitalised 'Father's House' and from there reconstructed the 'meaning'.

Admittedly Clarissa's dramatic agency is minimal, and the novel is not really concerned to demonstrate it. It is more concerned to present an ideal which will overcome all gaps of mediation. Richardson does, however, indicate the extent to which the ideal can move toward dramatic enactment, as in the allegorical letter, and the extent to which it must go, as in the need for Clarissa to set out her whole story in the cause of its own truth. One difference of Richardson's novel from later novels must be noted; Clarissa's agency, her activity in the sign system, is not necessary for her own personal completion or development. It is undertaken in order to educate others, and to provide them with an example. From an outside point of view, the construction 'Clarissa' is a dramatic model which readers are expected to emulate. As an image of soul she is meant to awaken in readers a sense of the movements of their own souls, and so change the world.[19] After the Romantic Movement's re-emphasising of the difficulties imposed on realising the private self in public, as well as the new sense that 'soul' is not something given, but something that grows or evolves and requires cultivation or culture, activity in the public media systems becomes something that may well still serve the public, but it is seen to be necessary also for the realisation, or actualisation of the self. Self, which is the real subject of novels, is unlike soul only in that it requires completion in action. The new concern with subjectivity in the nineteenth-century novel does not eliminate dramatic matters; instead it makes the theatrical elements of the novel all the more important. Because of this fact, one can argue, as it is the purpose of this book to do, that there are recurrent structural elements in the novel. This structural argument does not commit one to arguing that all novels make the same use of the elements. Indeed the recurrence of structural elements is the one fact that allows one to perceive both continuity and change—or to perceive what is both novel about a novel, and what, at the same time, keeps it generic.

So Davis's claim that the novel in its beginnings does not show the interest that Elizabethan fiction does in the need for Idea to be embodied in Act is not quite true. It is true to say that the emphasis has changed and it is now 'soul' or 'mind' rather than a platonic Idea that is to be enacted, and this shift towards the individual personality is crucial for the origin of the novel, but the metaphorical clothing, drawn from the drama, remains the same. James Hogg's marvellous and curious fiction, *The Private Memoirs and Confessions of a Justified Sinner* is more of a romance, or secular parable or allegory than novel, but while it deals with character in terms of soul and the dangerous bargain that soul can make with the Devil, it is clearly on its way to conceiving of character and identity in wholly secular terms. As André Gide says in his eulogy of the book:

> But I doubt whether Hogg's personal point of view is that of true religion or whether it is not rather that of reason, common sense and a natural Tom Jones-like expansiveness, which is that of the 'justified sinner's' brother, whom the 'justified' murders. . . .[20]

Clearly, as Gide notes, all of Hogg's sympathy is with the 'normal humanity' of the murdered brother, and none with the brother, Robert Wringham, who is the 'author' of the journal. For this reason we can believe, as the text hints, that the work is a kind of parable meant to demonstrate not the danger of toying with the Devil—not meant, that is to say, to engage in metaphysical dispute—but to show the dangers of dressing oneself in the garb of dangerously rigid dogma.

The creed to which Robert Wringham holds is an extreme Calvinistic Antinomianism, especially the belief that one is justified in everything if one belongs to the elect. This doctrine amounts to a kind of passivity, since it denies the validity of any act. The just, being promised salvation from before the beginning of the world, can neither earn salvation by any act of his own, nor lose it. The murdered brother, George, is an active and vital youth, playing tennis, drinking, carousing and living a life 'spontaneous, gay, rich in possibilities'.[21] Robert, by contrast, never acts from a personal centre at all, and can therefore be fooled by the devil's tricks. Blind to his real motive, a 'jealous and brooding hatred and, moreover, with the desire of getting hold of the elder brother's share of their father's inheritance', he puts on the apparent motives of religious duty in order to rid the world of an evildoer. His motivation comes from outside, and is provided him by the 'Devil'. What this means in secular terms is that the person who does not spontaneously act from inner motives, will act from motives acquired as a costume, and we see the characteristic results of donning such clothes

passively: they began to eat out further any inner resources Robert
Wringham might have had.

Early on, Wringham sings a hymn which he privately directs towards his
hated brother, with reference to his use of profane language:

> As cursing he like clothes put on,
>   Into his bowels so,
> Like water, and into his bones
>   Like oil, down let it go.[22]

The image here is of language behaving like a shirt of Nessus and burning
inwards; ironically this is the fate suffered by Robert himself. He puts on the
language of external justification, and it destroys his soul. Defined by his
black clothes, indicating a lack of projection of vitality, Robert himself
becomes increasingly hollow: 'my bosom became as it were a void, and the
beatings of my heart sounded loud and hollow in it'.[23] As a result he
becomes cannibalistic of the vitality of his brother. On Arthur's Seat, in
Edinburgh, George sees the figure of his brother menacing him: 'Its eyes
were fixed on him, in the same manner as those of some carnivorous animal
fixed on its prey . . .'.[24] Robert rejects all human activity and regards 'the
righteousness of man as filthy rags'.[25] When he encounters the devil he
makes a characteristic error, mistaking the clothes for the 'man': '"What
was my astonishment on perceiving that he was the same being as myself.
The clothes were the same to the smallest item."'[26] In an interjected tale,
Robert's servant, Penpunt, warns him of the Devil's tricks. Two demons,
disguised as 'corbies', are overheard planning to make a meal on the
overzealous citizens of Auchtermuchty: '"I fear they will be o'er weel
wrappit up in the warm flannens o' faith, an clouted wi' the dirty duds o'
repentance, for us to mak a meal o'"', says one. Nevertheless, they make an
attempt to fool the townsfolk by turning their clothes, or their strengths,
against them. They are saved at the last minute by one who pulls aside the
minister's robe to reveal the cloven foot. From that day to this the folk of
Auchtermuchty can hardly be made to listen to a sermon.

When Robert is being closely pursued by the officers of the law he is
'saved' by his 'friend', who changes 'habits' with him and says '"There is a
virtue in this garb"'.[27] Hogg's parable, or allegory, given such a significant
recurrence of metaphors of clothing, is not too difficult to make out. Robert
puts on virtue like clothing. Hogg believes that virtue is a more manly
and active thing that must arise from within and be projected outwards
in action. Robert quickly discovers the dangers of reversing the proce-
dure:

> if there were virtues in the robes of the illustrious foreigner, who had
> without all dispute preserved my life at this time: I say, if there was any
> inherent virtue in these robes of his, as he suggested, this was one of their

effects, that they turned my heart towards that which was evil, horrible, and disgustful.[28]

Robert's fate is finally sealed when he pronounces an equivocal prayer that he has been taught by the devil. His attitude to clothing is reflected in his attitude to language; he says the words as if they were mere signs without meaning, and discovers that he has given himself up to be devoured by demons.

If we turn to Dickens, particularly *Bleak House*, we find the central group of meanings that cluster around the notion of cannibal clothes reappearing. Dickens, of course, conceives of something like soul and believes in it more seriously than does Hogg, perhaps. Nevertheless he analyses evil, and good, in quite secular or social terms. Love, of course, is a solution that one can denominate either metaphysical or social, and it does not really matter what one thinks on this point. Dickens' analysis of the equivocal nature of signs and fictions will be considered at length in Chapter 5. Mention is made there also of the central philosopher of clothes for the nineteenth century, Carlyle. It might just be mentioned here that, obviously, Carlyle did not invent the metaphor of 'clothing' for symbolism, or for the idea that the whole of the material world is a kind of clothing for the divine spirit. One can sense the origin in German idealism of some of his thought, and one is aware of the tremendous influence on English novelists of Carlyle's use of the metaphor. Dickens' debt to Carlyle continues to be demonstrated[29] and one can see that Thackeray was influenced by Carlyle as were lesser novelists like Charles Kingsley in, for instance, *Alton Locke*. The other source of the clothing metaphor for Carlyle is, however, Swift, in the well-known passage from a satire on a strange new sect:

> The Worshippers of this Diety had also a System of Belief, which seemed to turn upon the following Fundamental. They held the Universe to be a large *Suit of Cloaths*, which *invests* every Thing. . . . To conclude from all, what is Man himself but a *Micro-Coat*, or rather a compleat Suit of Cloaths with all its Trimmings? As to his Body, there can be no dispute; but examine even the Acquirements of his Mind, you will find them all contribute in their Order, towards furnishing out an exact Dress: To instance no more; Is not Religion a *Cloak*, Honesty a *Pair of Shoes*, worn out in the Dirt, Self-Love a *Surtout*, Vanity a *Shirt*, and Conscience a *Pair of Breeches*, which, tho' a Cover for Lewdness as well as Nastiness, is easily slipt down for the Service of both.[30]

Sartor Resartus employs the same tone as does *A Tale of a Tub*, perhaps the only tone justifiable for a disquisition on the philosophy of clothes. The present work may well have the unenviable distinction of being one of the few non-ironic treatments of the subject.

Part of our argument is that the world defined merely by clothing, to the detriment of the inner world of soul, or mind, or heart (the word associated with the Victorian writers), is cannibalistic. At the risk of pedantic thoroughness one ought to mention the fact that Swift, in *A Modest Proposal*, suggests as a solution for those who view moral problems in superficial terms the practice of cannibalism. In Dickens, at any rate, the matter is clearly put. The official world, the artificial and established world of society is a world defined by its language, its clothing, its 'roles', and it is therefore cannibalistic.

Obviously drawing from Carlyle's discussion of 'dandyism' in *Sartor Resartus*, *Bleak House*[31] is Dickens' own analysis of the way the world wears its clothes. Like Carlyle, he is no sansculottist even though he perceives the evils of life in terms of the clothes that are worn. The point that both Carlyle and Dickens make is that clothes must be worn, especially the clothing of words that give presence to thought, but that they must be worn in the right way. What has happened is that the clothes have attained a frightening degree of freedom. Carlyle's treatment of the philosophy of clothes will not be developed here, since, although he obviously influenced Dickens, Dickens himself has a coherent and complex vision of his own on the matter that has not often been analysed.

Mr Turveydrop is only the most visible embodiment of a theme that permeates the novel. Here is part of the description of this model of Deportment:

> He was a fat old gentleman with a false complexion, false teeth, false whiskers, and a wig. He had a fur collar, and he had a padded breast to his coat, which only wanted a star or a broad blue ribbon to be complete. He was pinched in, and welled out, and got up, and strapped down, as much as he could possibly bear. He had such a neckcloth on (puffing his very eyes out of their natural shape), and his chin and even his ears so sunk into it, that it seemed as though he must inevitably double up, if it were cast loose.[32]

Clearly if there is any man here at all, he is made by his clothes. Like the much more malicious Tulkinghorn and Vholes, Turveydrop is in an advanced state of Dandyism in which it is becoming impossible to differentiate between clothing and human flesh. As Esther notes, '"As he bowed to me in that tight state, I almost believe I saw creases come into the whites of his eyes."' Like Sir Leicester, who is introduced as a well-dressed gentleman in a 'blue coat with bright buttons always buttoned',[33] Turveydrop lives off the labour of others. Turveydrop is especially parasitical in his relationship to Prince and Caddy. The difference in Sir Leicester is that his severe shell does apparently mask a genuine regard for Lady Dedlock, and when she is lost he shows genuine remorse. Under Turveydrop's clothes there is only self-regard.

Sir Leicester, however, lives at the centre of a widespread social

Dandyism, which has taken a different form since the time of the Regency buck has passed:

> There is no beau whom it takes four men at once to shake into his buck-skins, or who goes to see all the executions, or who is troubled with the self-reproach of having once consumed a pea. But is there Dandyism in the brilliant and distinguished circle notwithstanding, Dandyism of a more mischievous sort, *that has got below the surface* and is doing less harmless things than jack-towelling itself and stopping its own digestion, to which no rational person need particularly object?
>
> Why, yes. It cannot be disguised. There *are*, at Chesney Wold this January week, some ladies and gentlemen of the newest fashion, who have set up a Dandyism—in Religion, for instance . . . . There are also ladies and gentlemen of another fashion, not so new, but very elegant, who have agreed to put a smooth glaze on the world, and to keep down all its realities. . . On whom even the Fine Arts, attending in powder and walking backward like the Lord Chamberlain, must array themselves in the milliners' and tailors' patterns of past generations, and be particularly careful not to be in earnest, or to receive any impress from the moving age.[34]

The text then moves on to the well-known passages on Boodle, Doodle and Buffy, Cuffy, Duffy, all 'great actors for whom the stage is reserved'; all examples of moral and spiritual Dandyism.

Now this passage is not a mere extravaganza on Dickens' part; it is rather intended as an obvious announcement of a central theme for the novel, and it is carried through in detail, and extensively.

It is a very usual practice for Dickens to describe his characters in terms of their clothes of course, and there is no need to dwell on the fact except in order to show how metaphors of clothing work together and further to attempt what has not so often been attempted, to explain the meaning of these metaphors. In *Bleak House* both Tulkinghorn and Vholes can be characterised by the comment made by Lady Dedlock on Tulkinghorn alone: 'He is indifferent to everything but his calling. His calling is the acquisition of secrets, and the holding possession of such power as they give him . . .'.[35] One might note that Tulkinghorn is to be contrasted with Bucket in this, who says to George: '"Duty is duty, and friendship is friendship. I never want the two to clash."'[36] Bucket can pull off this combination because of his miraculous, almost magical powers, but perhaps one ought not to try to argue that such a separation of duty and friendship was Dickens' ideal. At least one can say that, unlike Tulkinghorn, Bucket has a calling but he manages also to have something, friendship, beyond that. Like Jaggers he is able to exist at the magical crossing point of the public and private worlds, where the tension between the two is productive of an access of power, a power quite unlike Tul-

kinghorn's because it works towards the publishing of secrets rather than
the hoarding up of them.

Vholes and Tulkinghorn are totally identified by their roles in society,
however, and the metaphors of clothing serve to inform us of the cost of
such an acquired identity. Vholes is more interesting in this respect,
although the rusty and uncommunicative clothing of Tulkinghorn is mentioned very often in the story.[37] The defence of Vholes' profession runs
something like this: eliminate lawyers and what becomes of the people who
are dependent on them, such as relatives:

> Are they to be shirt-makers, or governesses? As though, Mr. Vholes and
> his relations being minor cannibal chiefs, and it being proposed to abolish
> cannibalism, indignant champions were to put the case thus: Make
> man-eating unlawful, and you starve the Vholeses![38]

Once again, we are faced with no mere casual metaphor, as we shall see.
Vholes is another example of Dandyism that has begun to operate beneath
the surface.

His clothing has been eating away his substance—at one point the text
defines ghosts as 'garments that have no substance in them'[39]—and as a
result he, and the others like him who are defined only by role, begin to eat
their fellows. We see Mr Vholes preparing himself for professional duties:
'Mr. Vholes, quiet and unmoved, as a man of so much respectability ought
to be, takes off his close black gloves as if he were skinning his hands, lifts
off his tight hat as if he were scalping himself, and sits down at his desk.'[40]
Clothing has all but become flesh. He stares at his client (Richard) 'as if he
were making a lingering meal of him with his eyes as well as with his
professional appetite'.[41] His lack of inner vitality, and the lack of resultant
expressive activity, is to be contrasted with Mr Jarndyce. Vholes has a
'buttoned-up half audible voice, as if there were an unclean spirit in him
that will neither come out nor speak out. . .'.[42] Esther makes the comparison: 'the one giving out what he had to say in such a rich ringing voice,
and the other keeping it in such a cold-blooded, gasping, fish-like
manner'.[43] Tulkinghorn shows the same parsimonious attitude to the expressivity of language, asking at one point for 'half a word' with Snagsby, as
if he were trying to save the other half.

One can also contrast the energetic George:

> What is curious about him is, that he sits forward on his chair as if he were
> from long habit, allowing space for some dress or accoutrements that he
> has altogether laid aside. His step too is measured and heavy, and would
> go well with a weighty clash and jingle of spurs.

Although he no longer wears the external insignia, George is clearly somehow a soldier in himself. He is the sort of man who fills out the clothes and

makes the mere uniform into a soldier. His physical presence suggests this metaphorical truth about him: 'his large manner, filling any amount of room . . . [and] his sounding voice'.[44] He is to be contrasted also with the world of the Pardiggles 'where charity was assumed, as a regular uniform. . .'.[45]

The cannibalistic career of Vholes will be considered further, but other characters require some attention. In one particular pair of characters, the Smallweeds, we see a possible origin for Beckett's Nagg and Nell who live in garbage buckets. In violent agitation, Grandfather pitches a cushion at Grandmother Smallweed and then collapses in his chair:

> The effect of this act of jaculation is twofold. It not only doubles up Mrs. Smallweed's head against the side of her porter's chair, and causes her to present, when extricated by her grand-daughter, a highly unbecoming state of cap, but the necessary exertion recoils on Mr. Smallweed himself, whom it throws back into *his* porter's chair, like a broken puppet. The excellent old gentleman being, at these times, a mere clothes-bag with a black skull-cap on the top of it. . . .[46]

Later he is nothing but 'a bundle of clothes, with a voice in it calling for Judy'.[47] The young Smallweed shows signs of an interest to rise in the world by emulating the clerk Guppy, indeed 'He dresses at that gentleman (by whom he is patronised), talks at him, walks at him, founds himself entirely on him.'[48] One is tempted to guess that Dickens was aware of the possible pun on the name and in the great world of Dandyism the small-weeds are merely the unmentionable underdress, the smallclothes—they are of course also garden weeds. Smallweed senior is related to Mr Krook, the unofficial Lord Chancellor, by marriage. The usurer and the hoarder of documents are similar in their secret retentiveness, and in their characterisation. Mr Guppy, trying to wake the sleeping Krook, finds that 'it would seem as easy to wake a bundle of old clothes, with a spirituous heat smouldering in it'.[49] The self-immolation of this bundle of clothes prefigures the self-immolation of the Court of Chancery (the actual burning of which lies behind the story).

Clothing plays an important part in the plotting of *Bleak House* as well as in the presentation of character. The French maid, Hortense, signals her defection from Lady Dedlock's service by removing her shoes and returning to the house barefoot through the grass. Shortly after this symbolic indication that she has changed her role, has doffed her livery, she appears at Tulkinghorn's in Lady Dedlock's veil and gown and sufficiently fools poor Jo who believes he is seeing the same lady he took to the miserable burying ground of Nemo. Here, Lady Dedlock's change of clothing is linked thematically with her plight of imprisonment in one class while her lover and the father of her child has lived and died in another. She comes as close as she can to him by briefly adopting a change of clothing. When she finally takes flight, she changes clothes with the miner's wife and for a time throws the ingenious Bucket off her trail. Bucket himself has an unusual suit of clothing, very much like a magical robe, from which he can produce such things as a pair of handcuffs to slip onto George. When Smallweed and company beset Sir Leicester, intending blackmail, Bucket turns out to be the one in possession of the essential bundle of letters from Lady Dedlock to her dead lover: 'Mr. Smallweed looks, with greedy eyes, at the little bundle Mr. Bucket produces from a mysterious part of his coat, and identifies it as the same.'[50] As he is able to work some mysterious magic at the boundary crossing of public and private life, so it is appropriate that Bucket should have magic clothes.

One can take another another step towards understanding clothing by recalling that clothing is appearance, and since appearance can be misleading it requires interpretation. It is sometimes difficult to tell whether the figure before us is a man or a hollow suit of clothes (a hypocrite); we must learn to read what the surface tells us, for to ignore the signs is perilous; but equally we must learn to interpret the signs in order to see beyond them. This is where the whole theme of reading, or of learning to read (Krook) and the deciphering of documents is relevant. The documents of the Court of Chancery are a hollow suit of clothes and for this reason they will never be deciphered. No matter how much signification the court produces, none of the documents will be found to have any underlying meaning.

J. Hillis Miller in his introduction to the Penguin edition of *Bleak House* discusses this theme of documentation and interpretation and argues that the novel itself is a document like all others, like those of Chancery, and since no document is ultimately decipherable, he believes, the meaning of *Bleak House* lies in its irresolution.[51] This completely perverts the sense of the novel; the clothing of language of the novel, even though it is fiction, can be trusted precisely because it is not hollow, it is filled from within with imaginative vision. This means that unlike the hollow documents of Chancery, it can be deciphered and understood.

There are two good readers in the novel (perhaps three, if we include Jarndyce, who sees through Esther's intention to love him and discovers her suppressed love for Woodcourt): Esther and Inspector Bucket. Esther claims to have guessed at Jarndyce's intent to set up Woodcourt in a house and practice (she doesn't yet see to the depths of his intent), and Jarndyce says, '"What a Dame Durden it is to read a face!"'[52] Esther is guilty of some misreading here, but that is because Jarndyce is playing at being a benign hypocrite, not letting his left hand know what his right doeth. The fullness of his love and generosity will inevitably appear. By contrast, the good intentions of the speechless, stricken Sir Leicester, who wants to recover Lady Dedlock, require the utmost in interpretation. Bucket makes out everything:

'Bring it here, Sir Leicester Dedlock, Baronet? Certainly. Open it with one of these here keys? Certainly. The littlest key? *To* be sure. Take the notes

out? So I will. Count 'em? That's soon done. . . . Take 'em for expenses?
That I'll do, and render an account of course. Don't spare money? No I
won't.

The velocity and certainty of Mr. Bucket's interpretation on all these
heads is little short of miraculous. Mrs. Rouncewell, who holds the light,
is giddy with the swiftness of his eyes and hands, as he starts up, furnished
for his journey.[53]

As a reader Bucket can bring things up from below the surface, even when
the web of signals is as flimsy as that given out by the stricken Sir Leicester.
It is the vital dichotomy in Bucket that makes him such a good reader and
interpreter. He balances private life and duty, and this balance is suggested
by his ability to bring the necessary secrets out of the mysterious pockets of
his clothing. Similarly, he has an eye both for the surface of the signs, and
for what the signs must be and mean given the personal situation of the
signaller. He can imagine himself in Sir Leicester's situation and imagine
what he himself would be trying to signal in such a case. He has an eye for
the speaker's meaning and because of this the torn rags of the message itself
do not hinder him from extracting the meaning and acting upon it.

Krook, of course, is exactly the opposite and believes that the rags and
rubbish of documents that he collects are somehow in themselves magical
and contain what he needs to know. The point about his laborious attempts
to learn how to read and write is that they are completely misdirected. The
signs he wishes to interpret are always and forever empty because, as
documents of Chancery, they are not the surface residue of an intent to
communicate: they contain no personal speaker's meaning. The more
Krook tries to don the mere clothes of communication without the spirit of
human contact, the more likely is he to destroy himself. Krook's spontaneous combustion is an image of auto-cannibalism as is suggested by the
grim images of the air around his shop after his death, laden with the grease
and smell of over-cooked chops. Having cloaked himself in the hollow rags
of Chancery documents and having become identified with them, he must
suffer the destruction inherent in such clothing. That Krook would not be
better off for merely learning the formal signs of language is suggested by
the happier fate of the ungrammatical but loving Charley, Esther's maid.

By means of a pun Dickens makes the connection between the world of
Chancery (which is, of course, a pun in itself on 'chance') and the image of
the hollow and devouring clothes. It is Richard who is consumed by becoming entangled in the complex suit of Jarndyce vs. Jarndyce, and he himself
points to the fundamental mistake he made early on: ' "I was born into this
unfinished contention with all its chances and changes, and it began to
unsettle me before I quite knew the difference between a suit at law and a
suit of clothes. . ." '.[54] Jarndyce himself, by contrast, seems at one point to be
capable of a kind of sartorial murder: 'he would have strangled the suit if he
could.'[55] Vholes admits that Jarndyce 'was not active in it' (the suit). Richard

puts on the one suit in which it is fatal to try to act; it is really a shirt of
Nessus and leads inevitably to inward burning or consumption. Ironically,
by remaining passive in the suit, Jarndyce virtually escapes the evil effects
of such clothing (as has been noted, he is perhaps blinded for a time to the
discrepancy in age between himself and Esther; Esther's comment about
Fatima and Bluebeard could possibly be taken as a hint of the direction
Jarndyce would have gone had he ever been active in the suit). The Chancery suit that Richard attempts to wear actively, is a kind of writing and it
leaves its mark on him, as Esther suggests:

> His hopefulness had long been more painful to me than his despondency;
> it was so unlike hopefulness, had something so fierce in its determination
> to be it, was so hungry and eager, and yet so conscious of being forced
> and unsustainable, that it had long touched me to the heart. But the
> commentary upon it now indelibly written in his handsome face, made it
> far more distressing than it used to be.[56]

We have to imagine that it is because he has more heart and because he
makes a more personal commitment to donning the suit that Richard suffers
from its indelible writing, whereas Vholes apparently does not. Vholes and
Tulkinghorn both seem to earn a slight edge of longevity in the suit as a
result of their professional indifference to its outcome. In a sense, Vholes
does not exist as a person at all, but as we have seen, even his flesh is now
only a part of the whole garment. As long as the garment lasts, Vholes will
last. The particular suit of Jarndyce and Jarndyce suffers the fate of cannibal
clothes: they eventually run out of external sustenance and have to devour
themselves. As Woodcourt says, 'the suit lapses and melts away'. As long
as there is a Chancery, however, there will be another suit for such as
Vholes; for example, as Dickens says in his preface, 'There is another
well-known suit in Chancery, not yet decided, which was commenced
before the close of the last century, and in which more than double the
amount of seventy thousand pounds *has been swallowed up on costs.'* (My
italics.) Before it turns on itself the voraciousness of such suits finds much
external fodder. As an 'agent' of the suit, Vholes seems to be finishing off
Richard:

> As he gave me that slowly devouring look of his, while twisting up the
> strings of his bag, before he hastened with it after Mr. Kenge, the
> benignant shadow of whose conversational presence he seemed afraid to
> leave, he gave one gasp as if he had swallowed the last morsel of his
> client, and his black buttoned-up unwholesome figure glided away to the
> low door at the end of the Hall.[57]

Vholes, however, is not the only one eating Richard. Richard himself, by
having put on the suit and identified himself with it, becomes the 'agent' of

his own destruction, as we see in perhaps the most significant and grue-some image in the novel, which occurs just as Richard is about to 'begin the world':

> Allan had found him sitting in the corner of the Court, she told me, like a stone figure. On being roused, he had broken away, and made as if he would have spoken in a fierce voice to the Judge. He was stopped by his mouth being full of blood, and Allan had brought him home.[58]

The full poetic meaning of this image is not available to us except by means of a careful consideration of the complexly mixed metaphor at work in this novel. The fact that the dominant metaphor of the novel is a com-posite one is not, perhaps, surprising, given the theme we have found conveyed by it. Without a doubt, much of the meaning of the novel is immediately available to the average reader and the sophistication of critical interpreters seldom adds much to the average reader's understanding of a great work. The average reader may have been thought of by Dickens as someone like the ungrammatical Charley, who would neither notice nor need the literary awareness needed to produce such a tale. The heart would respond to the heart that informs the signs. Over-exacting critical interpre-tations, that find in every little sign or twitch in print some symbolical pattern, may be likened to the blindness of Krook looking for the secret. The best one can hope is that sophistication at the surface of the text will be self-consuming in the long run. The present exercise might be thought to belong to the same category, and perhaps it does. It is not part of the present argument, nor, as we shall see in the Chapter on *Dombey and Son*, part of Dickens', that clothes and signs and surfaces are negligible. Nor can it be assumed that the heart can always work infallibly, since the world is after all a world of signs and one must learn to be active in it somehow—the magic of Bucket, like that of the artist in words, points the way—and be an interpre-ter. The end result of such interpretation of the surface linguistic clothing of the text should not, however, be out of spirit with what one *feels* Dickens' message to be. If the interpretive activity is surprising or new, it is so by showing us what we, in a sense, already know. It can also show us with satisfaction that the complex surface of the text does adequately coincide with what we take to be the spirit of the book. Which is to say, it shows us that Dickens was a careful artist. This does not mean what it once might have been thought to mean: that there is a consistency in every sign or symbol in the book. Indeed, part of the message of the artistry of Dickens is that the signs cannot contain everything; at best they can point, and the reader is the one who has to see, and to see beyond. A mixed metaphor might therefore be thought of as part of the method; or as something that would appeal to Dickens because of the comic fact of its apparent inade-quacy, which his imagination would make work by fleshing out the clothes with meaning from the inside.

The images of 'cannibal clothes' prove quite conclusively that Dickens' attitude to society is as unlike what is often taken to be that of the Victorian novelists as it possibly could be. His first assumption is obviously that institutions are a threat to the inner freedom of heart which is the one essential value. His attitude is not a simplistic anti-social one either. Institutions are obviously necessary. The solution to this paradox lies in the nature of the relationship of the individual to the clothing of civil life. He must be active in them. *Bleak House* shows us the limit of personal activity as a means of saving oneself, however; the clothes of Chancery, its language and its suits, ought not to be put on at all, but ought to be allowed to consume themselves and ultimately be replaced by new clothes. Dickens, like Teufelsdrockh perhaps, is 'content that old sick Society should be deliberately burnt (alas! with quite other fuel than spice-wood); in the faith that she is a Phoenix; and that a new heavenborn young one will rise out of her ashes!'[59] For some reason it is surprising, still, to the modern sensibility to discover that the Victorians had such a Modern conception of society. If we look to one of the first of modern novelists, Conrad, we discover that his analysis of the relationship of the individual to society is very similar to that of Dickens. Naturally enough, his tale is dressed in different clothes and speaks to a different sensibility. Beneath the clothing of the particulars, however, we come once again upon a structuring spirit that seems to be an essential part of the working of the imagination in language.

T.S. Eliot's use of *Heart of Darkness* in his poem 'The Hollow Men' proves slightly misleading if we try to go back to the novel from the poem. Eliot quotes the native's line, '"Mistah Kurtz,—he dead"', and usually the poem is taken to mean that while most modern men are merely old clothes upon old sticks, as Yeats has it, or 'stuffed men', there are some, like Kurtz, who have at least the energy to commit themselves to a vision of evil and by this indirection indicate the opposite pole and challenge of the spiritual life to those left behind. The point of this is that it suggests that Kurtz is not one of the hollow men, whereas in the terms we have been using thus far, and in the terms that Conrad uses, it is precisely because Kurtz is hollow at the core that he is led into extremities. Like Lord Jim, Kurtz has ability in the abstract; he is a 'universal genius' and can do anything that falls to hand. Which is to say that he is an opportunist.

Kurtz comes to the Congo as the promising representative of a new breed of trader; he is virtually a missionary, only coincidentally looking for ivory. Kurtz, however, has been far more formed by the underlying principles of his culture than he is aware of. As an opportunist, he has dressed himself in the clothing of his society and the clothing has worked itself inwards to become his essence: his inner identity has become that of the company man; his one motive is to exploit for economic gain. Part of the meaning of his final summation, that so impresses Marlow, is that he recognises the horror of his own self-delusion; he comes to see that the rhetoric in which he has dressed his enterprises has in fact been hiding a dark heart. Briefly, at the last moment of his life, he looks inward and admits the hollowness of his being and at this point, by making this judgement on himself, asserts himself privately, against the rhetoric of the company, and so achieves the possibility of becoming a 'full' human being.

Marlow himself is shaken to the core by the revelation of the Congo, and returns to tell the tale in Europe. As in the case of Jim, Marlow takes the meaning of another's life and gives it significance in the context where that meaning and significance are most necessary. The lateness of Kurtz's significant enunciation is partly compensated for by Marlow's tale. The message of the tale is that Europe had inappropriately tried to dress the Congo in European costume. Marlow learns that the cannibals of the jungle are human after all, and have possibly the advantage of being naked. They can at least see themselves, and can see the dark heart that beats in all men. Europeans are blinded to this inner darkness by the rhetorical clothing they wear. Surprisingly, it is the cannibals who show the most restraint because, one must assume, they have lived closer to the wild source of energy and therefore know more about controlling it. European forms have lost touch with their content. Rituals of civilisation no longer serve to transmute the primal energy into culture, or art. Instead, Europeans wear the trappings of culture and 'higher' goals, in order to carry on the robbing of their fellow men in the Congo. Marlow's transformation is indicated by his appearance as a 'Buddha preaching in European clothes'.[60] His task, and Conrad's, is to attempt redress by instilling a new spirit in the old clothes.

As soon as he joins the company, Marlow begins to feel an impostor; partly because the venture is dressed in false rhetoric:

> It appeared, however, I was also one of the Workers, with a capital—you know. Something like an emissary of light, something like a lower sort of apostle. There had been a lot of such rot let loose in print and talk just about that time . . .[61]

With his characteristic incisiveness Marlow ventures 'to hint that the Company was run for profit'. It is this underlying conflict between actual motive and enuciated ideal that destroys Kurtz. At first, for Marlow, Kurtz is a word;[62] he becomes finally a voice, a voice noted for its eloquence. This eloquence is ultimately replaced by a simple and uncomplicated sentence: '"The horror!"'. Marlow notes the eloquence of Kurtz's report: '"It was eloquent, vibrating with eloquence, but too high-strung, I think."' '"This was the unbounded power of eloquence—of words—of burning noble words."'[63] It does not take much of this to suggest that the eloquence is merely words; it is hollow rhetoric intended to cover up the company's motive. Kurtz has temporarily blinded himself to the real intent of the rhetoric and has made himself believe in it. His genius dresses itself in whatever robes fall to hand. The energy of the underlying motive cannot be held

down however, and blazes out 'like a flash of lightning': '"Exterminate all
the brutes!"'

What has not perhaps been said often enough about *Heart of Darkness* is
that it works towards the exploding even of ideals. Marlow's comment
about the Romans in Britain is probably meant to refer also to Kurtz:

> They grabbed what they could get for the sake of what was to be got. It
> was just robbery with violence on a grand scale, and men going at it
> blind—as is very proper for those who tackle a darkness. The conquest of
> the earth, which mostly means the taking it away from those who have a
> different complexion or slightly flatter noses than ourselves, is not a
> pretty thing when you look into it too much. What redeems it is the idea
> only. An idea at the back of it; not a sentimental pretence but an idea; and
> an unselfish belief in the idea—something you can set up, and bow down
> before, and offer a sacrifice to . . .[64]

This unusual passage in fact does a complete about turn. It begins by
espousing the Idea, but ends by suggesting that even an idea can be
destructive. This suggests that what makes Kurtz valuable to Marlow is
precisely the thing that destroys him. The apparent confusion of this is
partly cleared up by considering the way in which Kurtz wears his
ideals. Kurtz himself lacks some inner identity that would control the
operation of his ideals. He is an early type of the Greene evil-innocent character in whom the ideal operates without personal mediation and the
purity of the idea proves destructive of human values. Marlow concludes
that:

> Mr. Kurtz lacked restraint in the gratification of his various lusts, that
> there was something wanting in him—some small matter which, when
> the pressing need arose, could not be found under his magnificent
> eloquence. Whether he knew of his deficiency himself I can't say. I think
> the knowledge came to him at last—only at the very last. But the wil-
> derness had found him out early, and had taken on him a terrible
> vengeance for the fantastic invasion. I think it had whispered to him
> things about himself which he did not know, things of which he had no
> conception till he took counsel with this great solitude—and the whisper
> had proved irresistibly fascinating. It echoed loudly within him because
> he was hollow at the core. . . .[65]

It is because of this inner lack, this absence of personal identity not
acquired externally, that ideals operate evilly through Kurtz. Kurtz is in a
curious sense passive; he is a medium for the operation of a certain rhetoric
and certain ideals that are being used for other ends. This inner absence is
given significance in the novel by the number of times it is repeated and the
force with which it is stressed:

The mind of man is capable of anything—because everything is in it, all the past as well as all the future. What was there after all? Joy, fear, sorrow, devotion, valour, rage—who can tell?—but truth—truth stripped of its cloak of time. Let the fool gape and shudder—the man knows, and can look on without a wink. But he must at least be as much of a man as these on the shore. He must meet that truth with his own true stuff—with his own inborn strength. Principles won't do. Acquisitions, clothes, pretty rags—rags that would fly off at the first good shake. No; you want a deliberate belief. An appeal to me in this fiendish row—is there? Very well; I hear; I admit, but I have a voice, too, and for good or evil mine is the speech that cannot be silenced.[66]

In part this 'inborn' strength is acquired in a special way; it grows within one as a result of work:

'I like what is in the work—the chance to find yourself. Your own reality—for yourself, not for others—what no other man can ever know. They can only see the mere show, and never can tell what it really means.'[67]

Inborn here seems equivalent to self-born; it is achieved by individual effort and not acquired by heredity.

As Marlow says, the possession of a personal voice is the one thing requisite, and it is the thing which finally wins Marlow over to Kurtz. The way this is put in the text suggests that it is not the fact that Kurtz understands his failure at the end that is important, but rather that he can speak out his understanding: '"This is the reason why I affirm that Kurtz was a remarkable man. He had something to say."'[68] It is not, then, Kurtz's remarkable qualities nor his universal genius nor his belief in an Idea that is impressive; it is that when the clothes are stripped off he can discover a personal voice.

As with other characters we have considered, the commitment of himself to an external ideal, to an acquired suit of clothes, has had the expected consequences for Kurtz. He is hollow at the core and is therefore in need of filling; he is hungry. When Marlow first sees Kurtz, this is what he sees: '"I saw him open his mouth wide—it gave him a weirdly voracious aspect, as though he had wanted to swallow all the air, all the earth, all the men before him."'[69] The point is repeated towards the end of the story:

I had a vision of him on the stretcher, opening his mouth voraciously, as if to devour all the earth with all its mankind. He lived before me; he lived as much as he had ever lived—a shadow insatiable of splendid appearances, of frightful realities; a shadow darker than the shadow of the night, and draped nobly in the folds of a gorgeous eloquence.[70]

Having identified himself with his clothing, with his eloquence and his ideals, he has chosen both hollowness and cannibalism. Kurtz himself has of course been a victim of a kind of cannibalism. His opportunism has led him temporarily to doff his European clothes in the jungle, to rid himself of the last vestiges of restraint and to don native dress and customs. His passivity, his acquiescence to these new clothes, gives the wilderness the power to consume not only his soul but his flesh as well:

> The wilderness had patted him on the head, and, behold, it was like a ball—an ivory ball; it had caressed him, and—lo!—he had withered; it had taken him, loved him, embraced him, got into his veins, consumed his flesh, and sealed his soul to its own by the inconceivable ceremonies of some devilish initiation.[71]

There is one qualification that needs to be made to all of this in order to make Conrad's vision more fully accessible. Kurtz has turned obsessively egoistic and this has happened apparently as a result of his adhering to an external ideal; it has happened because, in fact, the ideal itself was hollow and the motives of the company were mixed, to say the least. This might suggest that Conrad views any form of external restraint as undesirable, but this is not so. We discover in a number of passages that Kurtz can go to extremities in the jungle precisely because of the absence of external laws; as the Harlequin says, '"there was nothing on earth to prevent him killing whom he jolly well pleased"'.[72] The jungle had 'beguiled his unlawful soul beyond the bounds of permitted aspirations'.[73] He is the victim of living in 'utter solitude without a policeman . . .'.[74] Kurtz '"had kicked himself loose of the earth. Confound the man! he had kicked the very earth to pieces."'[75]

What has happened is that Kurtz has embodied the Ideal; he has attempted to mix the finite with the infinite: this makes him extraordinary and it is what proves destructive, both to himself and to the ordinary human universe which by its nature is finite and imperfect. To use the jargon of the social psychologists, Kurtz has 'internalised' an ideal pattern. Conrad's point is that, whatever such an attempt may have in it of tragic heroism, it is not a viable way to the human community. Ideals must remain external to the self, so that they can be aspired to. Ideals are empty, and must be filled with individual human effort, with work in the ranks. Hence Marlow's unwillingness '"to affirm the fellow was exactly worth the life we lost in getting to him"'.[76] By internalising the ideal, by becoming it in its infinitude, Kurtz destroys himself and his expanded ego becomes cannibalistic. So Conrad does not choose one side of a necessary dichotomy. He does not favour the subjective individual against the restraint of society. External restraint is absolutely a necessity, in order to remind the individual where his subjectivity ends. It is essential, however, for an individual to meet this external fact with an inborn truth of personal identity. It is when someone tries to derive identity from external forms that he is on dangerous ground.

This point can be somewhat clarified by briefly considering two minor characters, one of whom has perhaps been the most puzzling figure of modern fiction, the Harlequin. First though, it is necessary to mention the one other European in the jungle who earns Marlow's respect, the company's chief accountant at the first station, whom Marlow calls 'this miracle'. This miracle of a man seems nothing more than a suit of clothes:

> When near the buildings I met a white man, in such an unexpected elegance of getup that in the first moment I took him for a sort of vision. I saw a high starched collar, white cuffs, a light alpaca jacket, snowy trousers, a clean necktie, and varnished boots. . . . He was amazing.[77]

It would be a mistake to allow this suit of clothes to confuse our understanding of the metaphors of clothing, and the theme of externals as related to personal identity. The clothes here represent an achievement; clothes do not keep themselves in immaculate condition in a jungle. The clothes of the chief accountant testify to the fact that he has maintained his character, his sense of himself, by working on something. It seems not to matter that his labour is absurd—not absurd when compared to the adventures of the Eldorado Expedition, of course—in fact one suspects that Conrad would be willing to admit that all human work is absurd but that it is still the one place where one can find and maintain one's 'inborn' strength. The keeping up of clothing, the maintaining of an appearance, is a kind of proof that there is someone in there doing the keeping up, as Marlow says:

> Moreover, I respected the fellow. Yes; I respected his collars, his vast cuffs, his brushed hair. His appearance was certainly that of a hairdresser's dummy; but in the great demoralization of the land he kept up his appearance. That's backbone. His starched collars and got-up shirtfronts were achievements of character.[78]

One best understands this clerk by seeing him as an inversion of the Malay steersmen of *Lord Jim*. Like them he keeps to his post. Unlike theirs, his cause (or context) is not a worthy one.

Marlow responds also to the Harlequin, if not quite with respect, then at least he finds himself '"seduced into something like admiration—like envy"'.[79] Like the chief accountant, the Harlequin is fond of well-kept books and this trait perhaps is what most earns Marlow's attention. Marlow's admiration is grudging, however, and we are reminded of the distance between youth and experience as it figures in *Youth*. Clearly, the Harlequin is an embodiment of youth and the 'unpractical spirit of adventure'. He has invested simply, and merely, in life: '"His need was to exist, and to move onwards at the greatest possible risk, and with a maximum of privation."'[80]

Also, clearly, there is a natural affinity between this youth, who seems to live on an Ideal, a 'modest and clear flame', and Kurtz. Opportunistic in his adventures, he has acquired his dress a bit at a time wherever he has happened to land on his feet. As in the case of Kurtz, the openness of personality of this youth seems about to have ironic consequences. He seems not to have worked in any ranks long enough to have acquired any uniform, nor possibly to have developed any quantity of inborn strength that comes from duty performed. As a result of the attractive unfixedness of his identity he has a certain freedom, but he has also a peculiar vulnerability. When he meets an extremist of ideals he is in danger of losing his freedom, and of losing his youth to the rigours of experience. He seems to have taken the ideal of selflessness to a dangerous extreme:

> I almost envied him the possession of this modest and clear flame. It seemed to have consumed all thought of self so completely, that even while he was talking to you, you forgot that it was he—the man before your eyes—who had gone through these things. I did not envy him his devotion to Kurtz, though. He had not meditated over it. It came to him, and he accepted it with a sort of eager fatalism. I must say that to me it appeared about the most dangerous thing in every way he had come upon so far.[81]

The danger is easy enough to comprehend. It lies in his passivity. Just as he accepts his costume as it falls to him from adventures seized opportunistically, rather than undertaken as a result of deliberate consideration, or meditation, so too he is on the verge of accepting Kurtz's influence. Which is to say that in his situation he is not at work trying to achieve significance by means of his own actions, or work, but is in that dangerous state of allowing his situation to dictate his meaning to him. The ideal of ego-absence becomes dangerous, because as it is openness to the world, it is also hollowness, and it provides the opportunity for the parasitic, cannibalistic Kurtz: '"It was curious to see his mingled eagerness and reluctance to speak of Kurtz. The man filled his life, occupied his thoughts, swayed his emotions."'[82] Marlow fears for the Harlequin because he is in the process of becoming a hollow shell, filled up from outside, the most dangerous condition of all for the soul.

This consideration of Conrad all but concludes this chapter, which has attempted to trace the ramifications of significant action, as defined in Chapter 1, from the beginnings of the novel right up to modern times. The discussion of Conrad is briefly taken up in Chapter 7 (with reference to *The Secret Agent*), and attempts to show that Conrad's analysis of the relationship between inner and outer, subjective and objective, derives primarily from the imaginative artist's attitude to language and the need to be active in one's signifying. His political ideas are corollaries of his idea of language itself. It is beyond the scope of the present book to trace our theme right up to contemporary times. Chapter 7 also deals briefly with some modern fiction.

Before moving on, it is perhaps necessary to note that the themes and metaphors we have been considering are all centrally related to the stress given in fiction to the fact that human identity is above all else a matter of active use of language. It is also therefore a focus on mediation. What the theme comes to is perhaps a statement that there must be an external system of signs, and we must suffer the fact that it will always be external to our subjectivity and will never, therefore, perfectly contain the impulses of our most private self. The fact that it is external, however, is the one condition our subjectivity needs to complete itself. The inner self must work to fill the external forms, to put on the clothing of language and appear in the world. The point of repeating this here is in order to allow us to have one brief look at two strange pieces of literature, *Wuthering Heights* and another short representative of the Gothic element in fiction, Sheridan Le Fanu's story 'Green Tea'.[83] The theme of this chapter emphasises the necessary separation of inner and outer, and the need for some connecting medium, and this is precisely the theme of 'Green Tea'. 'Green Tea' presents a mystery which is subsequently explained logically. A brief summary is all that is required here, although it cannot do full justice to the pleasure of the story. In the story, a clergyman is driven to a gruesome suicide as a result of being haunted by a horrible monkey, which follows him along streets and wherever he goes—a series of events of great delight to amateur Freudians, no doubt. The psychological explanation is completely off the mark, however. The suicide is explained in the denouement as the result of a physiological deterioration brought about by a chemical in green tea, a drink in which the clergyman was a great indulger. This chemical has a peculiar action. It 'excites the reciprocal action of spirit and nerve, and paralyses the tissue that separates these cognate functions of the senses, the external and the internal'. So death results from a breakdown in the tissue which separates—and therefore joins, or mediates—the inner and the outer. Clearly, this mediating tissue is a poetic metaphor for language itself.

At first sight it seems plain that *Wuthering Heights* is about anything except mediation. It ends with the unification of the two ghosts finally freed of the medium of their bodies, and so seems to be a Romantic tribute to the supremacy of spirit, or soul. In its treatment of soul, however, it is quite different from *Clarissa* and allows us to see the extent to which the novel changes as a result of the new evolutionary consciousness of the nineteenth century, most fully expressed and given a paradigm by Wordsworth's feeling that it is necessary to account for the *growth* of his mind. It is a common mistake to assume that the Romantic contribution to literature is only a new emphasis on subjectivity; equally important is their perception that self or soul, as permanent and unchangeable as it seems, as in *Clarissa*, is in fact something that appears in time—and in the clothing of time. Hence the importance in nineteenth-century literature of the theme of education.

Education, properly conceived, is the completion, the culturing and drawing out of something that is already there. Education is the process of realisation for the soul; it allows it and encourages it to fulfil itself by becoming embodied in action and social ritual. The one evil is education that reverses itself by forcing education down the throats of unwilling vessels, as in Dickens.

This theme is obviously related to the discussion in this chapter, which has shown the repeated necessity in a number of novels for the proper direction of flow, from inner to outer. It is this aspect of the theme that is appropriate to a consideration of *Wuthering Heights*, which is perhaps the profoundest study of permanence and change that our literature has produced. The fact that the souls of the two lovers finally roam free is a symbolical indication of Brontë's belief in the permanency of the individual self, and this is the aspect of the novel that usually attracts most attention. It does not take long for one to realise, however, that the book is shot through with change, and that Heathcliff's final change is one that brings him around finally to a righting of the relationship of inner to outer; a relationship which he has perverted by enslaving himself to an external condition and then trying to enforce other lives to follow his pattern by creating a determinist situation for them. In modern terms, Heathcliff attempts to apply a behaviourist or mechanist conception of identity and finally learns that man is spiritual.

One need only think of the plot of the novel to see just how much change takes place in the course of it. A new and strange infant is introduced into a household. The relationship between Heathcliff and Cathy seems to be a permanent one, when, as a result of an accident, Cathy changes. It is important to note that Cathy does change, in essence. When Lockwood arrives at Wuthering Heights and has a troubled dream in Cathy's bed, he is astonished to realise that the voice he has heard calling announces itself as Cathy Linton, despite the fact that the name carved on the sill is Cathy Earnshaw. The marriage with Linton therefore is not something that can be dismissed. The fact that Linton and the surface values he represents are at least as important to Brontë as is Heathcliff's romantic extremism is clearly indicated by the fact that the three of them are buried together. Heathcliff, too, changes, by running away and acquiring the trappings of the civilisation that Linton represents. At this state Heathcliff is at his most divided and most hypocritical. Nelly asks: '"Is he turning out a bit of a hypocrite, and coming into the country to work mischief under a cloak?"'[84] He dons a disguise in order to work his will, and not in order to complete the expression of a full subjectivity. Indeed it is at this point that Heathcliff completes the reversal of orders and, in the image we have used thus far, becomes hollow, as we shall shortly see. The process of change continues and Wuthering Heights is alienated from its former owners. Cathy dies; Heathcliff marries Isabella, who dies. Heathcliff reclaims his son and plans further evil at Wuthering Heights, only to find a queer change coming over himself. Finally his wilful plotting itself comes to an end and the natural process of change restores Wuthering Heights to Hareton and Cathy II.

Up to a point, Heathcliff seems to be in control of this process of change, but very shortly he is revealed to be the passive 'agent' of an independent and natural process of change. His mistake has been to try to identify himself too completely with the external forces of change. Such a claim seems to go against the usual argument about the novel, that Heathcliff is significant because he is identified with Nature. One can only say that the novel itself seems to bear out the present argument. It needs to be qualified by saying that Heathcliff identifies himself with the materiality of nature, with the conditions and situations, which themselves change, and he alienates himself from the spirit, represented by Cathy. By identifying with the mechanism he cuts himself off from the innerness of nature. Lockwood drops a hint about Heathcliff early on, when he notices him turn a look of hatred on young Cathy II, Mrs Heathcliff Jr: '"He turned, as he spoke, a peculiar look in her direction, a look of hatred unless he has a most perverse set of facial muscles that will not, like those of other people, interpret the language of his soul."'[85] It is only in part a look of hatred, as we know from the end of the novel where we discover that Heathcliff sees his Catherine reflected in the eyes of Cathy II. He has no control over his own material body and so it cannot interpret the language of his soul. In this unusual book, Catherine herself is Heathcliff's soul, as he is her body. The separation that has occurred between the two has left Heathcliff as a soulless body and Catherine as a bodiless soul. Catherine dies because 'The spirit which served her was growing intractable: she could neither lay nor control it.'[86] She has no body to control her spirit. This is the meaning of her famous statement '"I am Heathcliff."' In terms of the author's own life we can imagine that woman's soul expressing the need for the active embodiment in the world that seems to belong only to the sphere of men. The message that the soul is sending to the body is what Catherine calls out to Heathcliff and what Lockwood hears at the beginning of the novel, '"Let me in—let me in!"'

Heathcliff is unable to interpret this message until the last, when his will fades and he seems to allow the soul to enter. Towards the end of the novel, Nelly notes that the direction of Heathcliff's obsessive gaze turns from outside to inside: '"He was leaning against the ledge of an open lattice, but not looking out; his face was turned to the interior gloom."'[87] Further on she says:

> Now, I perceived he was not looking at the wall, for when I regarded him alone, it seemed, exactly, that he gazed at something within two yards distance. And whatever it was, it communicated, apparently, both pleasure and pain, in exquisite extremes, at least, the anguished, yet raptured expression of his countenance suggested that idea.

The fancied object was not fixed, either; his eyes pursued it with unwearied vigilance; and, even in speaking to me, were never weaned away.[88]

Clearly, as Heathcliff's will is withering away, Cathy has been allowed to enter the room. Hatch is surely right in arguing that the idea here is parallel to that of Schopenhauer and we see the Idea or Spirit being born (even Heathcliff's glance cannot be 'weaned' away from his source of new sustenance) to replace the World conceived as Will.

In order to complete this line of argument, one must argue that Will, Heathcliff's one strength, is in a sense external. The pattern of Heathcliff's life is set by his reflex reaction to the unpleasant situation in the Earnshaw home. His situation is very like that of Jane Eyre in the home of Mrs Reed. Jane's rebelliousness, like Heathcliff's, is obviously approved of by the author, but Jane escapes the danger of a personality fixed in mechanical rebelliousness by means of the education she receives at Lowood school from Helen Burns. Heathcliff does not achieve this freedom of the spirit until the end of his life. *Wuthering Heights* is an expanded version of the story of Jane Eyre from the red room experience up to the death of Helen Burns. When Catherine responds to the surface delight of Thrushcross Grange life, Heathcliff believes her 'converted into a stranger by her grand dress'.[89] The result of this, as we have seen, is that he tries to convert himself into a stranger by donning the cloak of Linton's social ease. Nelly makes the first allusion to the Satanic path that Heathcliff embarks on by noting that he is 'fit for a prince in disguise'.[90]

Heathcliff then attempts to coerce fate by imprisoning the young Cathy and brutalising Hareton. He does this almost in a spirit of satanic experimentalism: Heathcliff 'had the hypocrisy to represent a mourner' at Hindley's funeral, and then seizes on Hareton: ' "Now my bonny lad you are *mine*! And we'll see if one tree won't grow as crooked as another, with the same wind to twist it!" '[91] Heathcliff perhaps begins to see his powerlessness when he observes that his own son, Linton, who represents only the bodily heredity of Heathcliff, has nothing of Heathcliff in him at all.[92] The externals of nature are full of change. The other irony is that Hareton does turn out more like Heathcliff than could have been expected, but the expected warping does not take place because despite Heathcliff's 'wind', Hareton is exposed also to the influence of young Cathy, who 'grew like a larch'. Hareton's own nature, under Cathy's influence, begins to transcend the intended physical determinism he has been subjected to:

His honest, warm, and intelligent nature shook off rapidly the clouds of ignorance, and degradation in which it had been bred; and Catherine's sincere commendations acted as a spur to his industry. His brightening mind brightened his features, and added spirit and nobility to their aspect—I could hardly fancy it the same individual. . .[93]

Hareton, unlike Heathcliff, attains true nobility by projecting an inward state rather than donning personal identity like a cloak. We can also recall Heathcliff's perverse facial muscles that will not interpret his soul. Nelly had warned Heathcliff about this potential reversal and the danger of allowing the body to dictate to the soul:

> O, Heathcliff, you are showing a poor spirit!. . . Don't get the expression of a vicious cur that appears to know the kicks it gets are its desert, and yet, hates all the world, as well as the kicker, for what it suffers. . . . A good heart will help you to a bonny face my lad . . .[94]

As soon as Heathcliff begins wilfully to respond to the externals of the situation that seems to be depriving him of Cathy, he stops expressing his internal feelings: 'Catherine and he were constant companions still, at his seasons of respite from labour; but, he had ceased to express his fondness for her in words. . .'.[95] By denying the natural expressivity of the soul, Heathcliff begins to damage the very power of language in him. Lockwood notices the inversion when he is invited by Heathcliff to 'walk in': '"The 'walk in,' was uttered with closed teeth and expressed the sentiment, 'Go to the Deuce!'"'[96] Lockwood also notes that Heathcliff has a 'laconic style of chipping off his pronouns, and auxiliary verbs'.[97] When he tries to order about the young Catherine II, she defies him and points to the dis-memberment Heathcliff has willed on himself: '"I'll not do anything, *though you should swear your tongue out*, except what I please!"'[98] Heathcliff has indeed attempted to swear his tongue out, as we see in the curse he pronounces over his dead love:

> And I pray one prayer—I repeat it till my tongue stiffens—Catherine Earnshaw, may you not rest, as long as I am living! You said I killed you—haunt me then!. . . Oh, God! it is unutterable! I *cannot* live without my life! I *cannot* live without my soul![99]

Heathcliff commits the sin of the Ancient Mariner, who is only released when he learns to bless the water snakes.

By willing the paralysis of his tongue, Heathcliff alienates himself from significant contact with his soul, and also wills his own inevitable defeat. It is only when his will dies that he will be able to speak again to Catherine and she will be able to come in to him once again. By willing the externalisation of his soul, Heathcliff wills himself into becoming an empty shell, or a hypocritical cloak, as we have seen. This hollowness has its usual results. In saying she will protect Isabella from the wrath of Heathcliff, Catherine says, '"I like her too well, my dear Heathcliff, to let you absolutely seize and devour her up."'[100] When Isabella and Earnshaw have locked Heathcliff out of Wuthering Heights, he breaks through the casement: 'His hair and clothes were whitened with snow, and his sharp cannibal teeth, revealed by

cold and wrath, gleamed through the dark.'[101] Heathcliff describes his
attitude to Linton, protected for the time being by Catherine's regard: '"The
moment her regard ceased, I would have torn his heart out, and drank his
blood!"'[102] Isabella tells Earnshaw of how Heathcliff treated him when he
was unconscious: '"his mouth watered to tear you with his teeth"'.[103] The
man possessed by a hollow will has, however, put himself in a position in
which he himself will be cannibalised, by words. He has lost power over
words because of his abnegation of spirit, the one thing that can fill words
from inside with meaning. Catherine has accused Heathcliff of being the
cause of her death:

> 'Are you possessed with a devil,' he pursued, savagely, 'to talk in that
> manner to me, when you are dying? Do you reflect that all those words
> will be branded in my memory, and eating deeper eternally, after you
> have left me? You know you lie to say I have killed you; and, Catherine,
> you know that I could as soon forget you, as my existence! Is it not
> sufficient for your infernal selfishness, that while you are at peace I shall
> writhe in the torments of hell?'[104]

Like a shirt of Nessus, Catherine's words will eventually eat their way
through the shell of denying will that Heathcliff has dressed himself in. In
this case the destruction will be benevolent, because, as the meaningful
words work their way inwards, they prepare a path for the re-entry of
Catherine, for the rebirth of spirit in Heathcliff. The process of change is
complete when it has worked its way with the material body of Heathcliff.
Finally reunited with himself, with his soul, Heathcliff–Catherine stand for
a complete human being.

The difference from *Clarissa*, is that while *Clarissa* seems to operate with
an idea of an unchangeable soul completely separate from the changeable
surface of social life—which is evil, as its best representative Lovelace
would seem to suggest—in *Wuthering Heights* we are closer to the world that
Hopkins describes when he says, 'Man's spirit will be fleshbound when
found at best. The soul needs to appear in the changeable surface forms of
life in order to complete itself; and similarly, in order not to become voracious and cannibalistic, the mutable surface forms of life need to be filled
from inside by spirit. Even released from their bodies, the spirits are not
quite disembodied. They do not fly off to some aetherial empyrean, but
remain as chthonic spirits of the ground. The conception of the self, or soul,
is quite different from the conception found in *Clarissa*, then, but the
metaphors we have been tracing prove particularly useful in allowing us to
perceive the way in which the novel can itself be an example of both
permanence and change; how it can remain generically interested in the
way in which men structure meaning into significant forms and yet keep
itself alive by being always something different. If the clothes change, the
spirit wearing them remains the same. All deriving from the fact that men

must use language in order to be themselves together, these metaphors testify to the one central message of the novel, and that is that the active spirit is primary, and that it must learn a kind of passive receptivity to the external clothing of the spirit. If this lesson is learned then a higher kind of activity or agency is opened up as the spirit of man regains the power to invest itself in the forms of time.

4 Agency and Scene in Jane Austen

Jane Austen might easily be taken as one of the hardest of test cases for a thesis that the English novel is concerned with expressivity and vital human agency rather than with accommodation to comfortable middle-class values. Of all her novels the most difficult for such purposes is *Mansfield Park*. It is virtually a critical dogma that this novel differs from the rest in that it shows no evidence of Austen's characteristic irony. For these reasons *Mansfield Park* is the obvious novel to consider with reference to the themes of irony and action. The purpose here is not to pick up all of the metaphors we have been encountering so far, but simply to demonstrate a continuity in the active spirit of the novel. The meaning of the novel reveals a consistency with the meanings we encounter in other novels by other authors. Fanny is a source of deep inner meaning, but she lacks significance. It is only when she begins to act in public, to give her meaning a form and shape in dramatic scenes, that her author's ironic eye is willing to rest.

One of the simplest meanings of irony is distance, and when it is asserted that *Mansfield Park* lacks irony what is usually meant is that there is no distance between Fanny Price and her creator. Fanny is seen as a moral centre who offers difficulty to those of us who will insist on reading the book from a modern standpoint, and it is precisely this prickly discomfort that leads Lionel Trilling to defend the book; it offers a challenge to contemporary ethical relativists. As he says, 'When we have exhausted our anger at the offense which *Mansfield Park* offers to our conscious pieties, we find it possible to perceive how intimately it speaks to our secret inexpressible hopes.' The hope he means is the hope that it is possible to discover 'in principle the path to the wholeness of the self which is peace'.[1] Marvin Mudrick too sees little complexity in the book, and perhaps little value as well. He says, 'its prevailing tone is grave, its issue unequivocal. Fanny— center of the action—is no heroine indulged, at an ironic distance, by the author; she demands our earnest sympathy, and on her own terms.'[2] Whatever we may come to believe about the accuracy of this judgement, it is the precise delineation of Austen's type of irony by Mudrick that attracts me here, and I believe it is possible to argue that Fanny is subject to Austen's characteristic treatment; she is treated with an ironic distance and at the same time she is indulged by her creator. It is the indulgence—that is, ultimate acceptance—that makes it difficult to spot the irony, which is never heavy-handed.

If Jane Austen treats Fanny ironically, then that must imply that there is a higher morality, that of the narrator with the ironic tone of voice or with the ability to structure ironic situations, that tests Fanny's morality. If a character is to be tested by a higher morality and yet ultimately indulged, the implication is that her wanderings from the higher code are never great and, further, that she is capable herself of developing a higher morality. Indulgent irony implies then that the central character will change, grow, develop, undergo a process of education in the novel. Indeed—as has often been observed—one of the central themes of the novel is precisely education. Sir Thomas's daughters Maria and Julia are highly educated; from a very early age they could put together the jigsaw map of Europe and 'repeat the chronological order of the kings of England' and 'of the Roman emperors as low as Severus . . .' and a great deal besides. Sir Thomas comes to lament this education; in fact he himself is educated in the course of the novel to the extent that he too is worthy of the author's indulgence:

> Here had been grievous mismanagement; but, bad as it was, he gradually grew to feel that it had not been the most direful mistake in his plan of education. Something must have been wanting *within*, or time would have worn away much of its ill effect. He feared that principle, active principle, had been wanting. . . .[3]

He discovers that his daughters 'had been instructed theoretically in their religion, but never required to bring it into daily practice'.[4] In contrast to Maria and Julia, Fanny has had little formal education, in her early life at least. Her girlhood in Portsmouth was far from the ideal of Rousseau, as we discover from a later scene in the novel, but Fanny does seem to have had time to develop the quality we see operative in her younger sister Susan, which is called a 'natural light of the mind'.[5]

Despite her lack of information, Fanny has what her cousins lack; she has inner formation. In this sense, then, she is a prime candidate for education in its proper sense, its root sense of drawing forth, drawing out. For although Fanny is not wanting within, there is a sense in which she is wanting without, or externally. She has, that is, the inner sense of principle which Sir Thomas speaks of, but the novel forces us to recognise that inner principle is not in itself enough; it must be *active*. Fanny is above all a passive character; she suffers but she does not act. At least she does not act readily. What she has to learn is not how to act properly, since she is proper enough; she must learn to act. This theme can only be made fully apparent by a close consideration of the question of drama and acting in the novel. Two central themes come together, that of the necessity for recognising a proper sense of education in drawing forth what is within, and that of the need for actively projecting good in the world. If these claims are true, then one must argue that Jane Austen's irony has an almost Chaucerian touch to it, in that she plays with scripture. Fanny's name might well be an echo of the passage from the first book of Peter which reads: 'But let it be the hidden man of the heart, in that which is not corruptible, even the ornament of a meek and quiet spirit, which is in the sight of God of great price.' Fanny is a meek and quiet spirit, but the novel suggests, with indulgent irony, that to have great price in the sight of God is not always enough for men and women, who have to live also in the sight of their fellow men. Here, then, is potentially the ultimate source of indulgent irony, the irony of discordance, or incommensurability which we find whenever principles of ultimate or absolute extension try to operate in a finite world of fallen men. This is what Leacock calls the irony of the disharmony of means and end, or ideal and practice, or simply the irony of human imperfection.[6]

From first to last Fanny proves that she has 'mental superiority'.[7] This means that, like a Jamesian heroine on whom nothing is lost, she has a sympathetic imagination which allows her always to comprehend what will be the effect on others of anything said in company. Edmund perceives that Fanny has 'great sensibility of her situation, and great timidity'.[8] It is perhaps too tempting to suggest that Fanny has an excess of sensibility over sense; the point though is that Fanny's virtuous sensibility is potentially a defect since too great a sensitivity to the scene can deprive an agent of the ability to act and so change the scene or redefine the situation. By the end of the novel we discover that Fanny does begin to act and that while Mansfield Park has improved Fanny, Fanny has also improved Mansfield Park. A free agent can redefine the scene, and the new scene makes possible more free acts. By contrast, Mary Crawford shows her superficiality, undoubtedly an attractive superficiality, in her unthinking comments. In the chapel at Sotherton she speaks wittily at the expense of clergymen, completely unaware of the fact that Edmund is about to take orders. Mary speaks spontaneously and for effect, without regard to the feelings of others. It is impossible that she should not on occasion give offence, since she too has had a faulty education of the heart and has not been taught to feel by her stepfather the Admiral. She has not, to use Austen's often repeated phrase, been taught to 'feel as she ought'. The influence of a loving home seems to be all-important in the development of this sense of proper feeling. There is an important irony, therefore, in the fact that both Fanny and Susan, who have this natural mental superiority, are the children of another Frances who made a bad marriage, perhaps for romance, but certainly to displease her family. Fanny's mother is ironically akin to Lydia of *Pride and Prejudice*. Though she made a bad marriage, she brings up two children, more if we include William, Fanny's loving brother, who do embody the central moral quality in the novel: proper feeling.

Mary, because of this lack of sound education in the family, when she acts spontaneously must very often act corruptly. She acts on her feelings, and her feelings are bad. This is made most evident near the end of the novel when Edmund finally has his eyes fully opened. Mary's only comment on the flight of Maria and Henry Crawford is to lament not the offence, but the detection of it. She then goes on to regret that by his action Henry had forfeited Fanny, once again missing the point that Henry has proven himself to be inconsiderate of the feelings of others, and therefore shown himself to be unworthy of Fanny. As long as Henry's corruption goes undetected, Mary seems to believe it would be all right for him to marry Fanny, even though such an arrangement would in fact be equal to wishing Fanny misery at some future date when his corruption does manifest itself. Edmund's comment on Mary is worth noting:

> I do not consider her as meaning to wound my feelings. The evil lies yet deeper; in her total ignorance, unsuspiciousness of there being such feelings, in a perversion of mind which made it natural to her to treat the subject as she did. She was speaking only, as she had been used to hear others speak, as she imagined every body else would speak. Her's are not faults of temper. She would not voluntarily give unnecessary pain to any one, and though I may deceive myself, I cannot but think that for me, for my feelings, she would—her's are faults of principle, Fanny, of blunted· delicacy and a corrupted, vitiated mind.[9]

Mary Crawford has learned well enough how to put on an act in society so as to entertain and to please. Since her acting must either be superficial and inappropriate to the situation, or corrupt, since when she expresses her inner self she projects her inner 'vitiation', she can never be a good actor. But the phrase 'good actor' begins already to take on a double ring. The one whose act in the play of society will be 'good' in the sense of aesthetically pleasing over the longest time, most consistently, will be the one whose intentions or feelings or morality are good. The aesthetically good actor, if he is to last, must be also an ethically good man. It is possible also, therefore, that the ethically good man must learn how to be a good actor in the dramatic sense. Principle which is quiet and meek is not enough.

Let us consider briefly two exemplars of 'acting': Mrs Norris and Henry Crawford. The verbal and situational irony with which Austen treats Mrs Norris are, of course, devastating. The first chapter shows her in all her inconsistency as she promotes the plan for Fanny to come to Mansfield and then quickly shirks all responsibility for her niece. She does what she can to define a situation which will force inactivity and a sense of inferiority on Fanny by insisting on the difference between her and her cousins Maria and Julia. She actively asserts her judgements and proclaims for a fact her belief that to introduce Fanny into the Mansfield household is to risk no romance between her and either Edmund or Thomas. The situation as it develops turns out to be tellingly at odds with what Mrs Norris has decided it should be. One short statement of Mrs Norris's reveals fully for us the inverted categorical imperative on which she tries to operate: 'It is morally impossible. I never knew an instance of it.'[10] The moral lassitude of Lady Bertram is similar: 'Lady Bertram holding exercise to be as unnecessary for every body as it was unpleasant to herself; and Mrs. Norris, who was walking all day, thinking every body ought to walk as much.'[11] They try to make their own experiences and opinions serve as universal laws. It is no wonder then that the activities of Mrs Norris are so often at odds with what the situation requires. She never looks to see what the situation *is* because she is too busy trying to define it for others.

Fanny is just the opposite, of course: she is supremely aware of what the situation is at all times, but she does not act a full part in the situation, partly at least because she acquiesces in the definition of the scene promoted by Mrs Norris. When opinions are being aired about the newcomers to Mansfield, Mary and Henry Crawford, the narrator informs us:

> Few young ladies of eighteen could be less called on to speak their opinion than Fanny. In a quiet way, very little attended to, she paid her tribute of admiration to Miss Crawford's beauty; but as she still continued to think Mr. Crawford very plain, in spite of her two cousins having repeatedly proved the contrary, she never mentioned *him*.[12]

This is polite reticence perhaps, a refusal to say anything unpleasant. But her refusal to say anything negative about Henry Crawford has slightly more worrying implications in another scene to be considered shortly. To complete the comparison of Fanny and Mrs Norris, we need only note what the narrator tells us about them with respect to innate ability to act in an important situation. One morning in Portsmouth Mr Crawford walks into the Price household unannounced. This presents Fanny with a situation in which she must do something herself to determine the course of affairs and we learn that 'Good sense, like hers, will always act when really called upon.' The momentous act in this case amounts to being able to 'name him to her mother, and recall her remembrance of the name, as that of "William's friend," though she could not previously have believed herself capable of uttering a syllable at such a moment.'[13] By contrast, Mrs Norris, at the news of Maria's flight with Crawford, finds her superficial shell of activity shattered: 'She had been unable to direct or dictate, or even fancy herself useful. When really touched by affliction, her active powers had been all benumbed.'[14]

The difference in magnitude between these two 'really' demanding calls on Fanny and Mrs Norris must indicate that while Jane Austen's view of Fanny's extreme sensibility is an indulgent one, it is not an unequivocal nor unhumorous one.

Mrs Norris's activity turns into passivity at the critical moment. Henry Crawford's agency, though, is not quite so flimsy nor so innocent in the long run. Henry, like his sister Mary, is not so obviously a negative character as is Mrs Norris because he acts with attention to the effect he is producing. He consciously cultivates an effective, dramatically effective, public image. He does not always try to dictate, define or direct the scenes in which he finds himself; he merely tries to steal the scene by upstaging all the other actors. Again, just to note the contrast, Fanny will learn to act according to the needs of the scene and the nature of the other actors in it. Henry is foremost in encouraging the staging of *Lover's Vows* at Mansfield, an event which is morally undesirable because of the absence of Sir Thomas who might disapprove, but more importantly it is undesirable because while Sir Thomas is at sea he is in mortal danger, and as Edmund says it is inappropriate for them to be entertaining themselves at such a time. The play is also inappropriate in that it might tend to foster an intimacy between Henry Crawford and the betrothed Maria, and force too early an intimacy of Edmund and Mary. It is important to note that it is the inappropriateness of the play given the larger situation, and not the mere fact of private theatricals, which is the question here. The play itself is an inappropriate act, given the current situation, or scene. The extraneous information that Jane Austen herself was an active participant in home theatricals ought to be enough to indicate that *Mansfield Park* is not tinged with an evangelical reaction against play-acting.

Indeed, at a later point in the novel, during an evening gathering at Mansfield Park, Henry Crawford reads from Shakespeare and the whole question of dramatic projection is considered more fully than in the earlier play scenes. Henry's ability stirs even Fanny:

> In Mr. Crawford's reading there is a variety of excellence beyond what she had ever met with. . . .—It was truly dramatic.—His acting had first taught Fanny what pleasure a play might give, and his reading brought all his acting before her again; nay, perhaps with greater enjoyment, for it came unexpectedly, and with no such drawback as she had been used to suffer in seeing him on the stage with Miss Bertram.[15]

Edmund too is greatly impressed by Henry's skill and he launches into a disquisition on the way in which knowledge of Shakespeare has worked its way into the very fibre of the character of the people of the nation. Further, he defends a spirit of improvement that is now abroad in the churches which would allow greater expressivity in clergymen reading the service. Older preachers '"to judge by their performance, must have thought reading was reading, and preaching was preaching"'. Edmund is obviously one who shares the beliefs of the improvers and puts the case tellingly: '"It is felt that distinctness and energy may have weight in recommending the most solid truths . . ."'. There is an obvious connection here with the other theme of 'improvement' which is raised on the visit to Sotherton, and I shall not discuss it here in full except to note that as Edmund is a believer in improvement, so too is Fanny, so long as improvement is not merely a fad and does not destroy something which is desirable from the past. Fanny and Edmund, and Jane Austen, it seems safe to say, have an Augustan sense of the value of improvement and they seem to accept Pope's beliefs

about landscape gardening and Art in general, that it is 'Nature to advantage dressed'.[17] The relevance for Fanny of Edmund's belief about expressivity needs to be stressed. She has as yet too little ability to act in society;
she may have the spirit of the most solid of truths inside her, but she needs
to learn the art of distinctness and energy in recommending that truth.
Henry, although superficially an actor, has nothing behind his words; he
can recommend with distinctness and energy, but he has nothing to
recommend and is therefore condemned to inconsistency and inconstancy.
His playing at life ultimately turns on him, when Maria takes seriously one
of his light comments to her, made because she is safely married, and
surprises him by leaving her husband for him. The man without a profound
and consistent conception of life's dramas will find his agency taken from
him by the scene itself when it turns actor.

In the section of the novel dealing with the staging of *Lovers' Vows*, we
find that the question of consistency and of turning actor is raised with
reference both to Edmund and Fanny. Edmund maintains an unpopular
opposition to the play, for the reasons outlined earlier, and then he lapses
into displeased silence when he sees that his objections have no effect. He is
at least somewhat satisfied that the production can apparently be limited to
the immediate family circle. The needs of casting the play and the shortage
of actors, however, soon lead to Thomas's insistence that an outsider, a near
stranger, be brought in to play 'Anhalt' opposite Mary Crawford.
Edmund's feelings for Mary convince him that he must now drop his
scruples and choose the lesser of two evils: by acting he will at least keep the
family circle closed and protect Mary from an undesirable and painful
intimacy with a stranger. The reader might well sympathise with Edmund
in his plight here, but Fanny is, quietly, condemnatory on hearing the news:

> He had told her the most extraordinary, the most inconceivable, the most
> unwelcome news; and she could think of nothing else. To be acting! After
> all his objections—objections so just and so public! After all that she had
> heard him say, and seen him look, and known him to be feeling. Could it
> be possible? Edmund so inconsistent. Was he not deceiving himself? Was
> he not wrong? Alas![18]

It turns out that Edmund is deceived in his love for Mary Crawford and the
veil is ultimately torn from his eyes. And Fanny's extreme moral con-
demnation does seem to have some pragmatic sense, since, despite
Edmund's motive in deciding to act, the other actors believe that 'he was
driven to it by the force of selfish inclinations only'. So this inconsistency,
no matter how well motivated, must to some extent compromise Edmund
as a moral agent on future occasions. Jane Austen may be wishing to make
us aware of the need for absolute principle here, but it may be equally
possible that she is suggesting that the scenes in which we find ourselves
may contain conflicting demands so that which role we should play is not

always easily ascertainable, and that on occasions when this conflict arises from a commitment of the heart, no one is capable of extreme, dogmatic moral consistency.

To make this point fully, one must consider Fanny's fate in the development of the staging of *Lovers' Vows*. On the night of the last rehearsal, as it turns out, Mrs Grant is unable to come. Fanny, although maintaining her refusal to act, has been drawn into several essential minor jobs and in fact has begun to enjoy her part in the business. In the absence of Mrs Grant the disappointment of the cast leads them to appeal once again to Fanny, if not to act, then to *read* the part for rehearsal. Fanny is made painfully aware that her presence at rehearsal has compromised her. By associating herself with the scene, she has been taking on definition as a participant at least, if not an actor. She hangs back however, unable to endure even the idea of reading the part. Edmund joins in the general request and she begins to be swayed: 'As they all persevered—as Edmund repeated his wish, and with a look of even fond dependence on her good nature, she must yield'.[19] And yield she does, in circumstances almost exactly like those of Edmund but a short while earlier. This inconsistency in Fanny, again perhaps a minor and excusable one—apart from Fanny's earlier private denunciation of Edmund—seems to be very consciously arranged by Jane Austen, and if we read the scene carefully it seems impossible not to conclude that Jane Austen has indeed been exercising her irony at Fanny's moral extremism. Not that there is anything wrong in Fanny's theoretical morality, but she has yet to learn how to act on this extreme principle of hers. If Fanny is deserving of the same moral strictures she applies to Edmund, perhaps she is due the same excuse. She yields to the demands of her situation because of an overwhelmingly complicating element, her affection for Edmund and his look of love for her. She too may be deceiving herself, but such deceit, for such a reason, although meriting ironic exposure, is a flaw so human as to be mildly indulged by the author. She does not let Fanny off completely however, since as soon as Fanny accedes to the request to read and takes up a script, Sir Thomas returns and the first volume of the novel ends dramatically with Fanny caught in the act.

There is a further point to be made about Fanny's earlier refusal to act. She refuses partly because of moral scruple, but the point is made that she refuses because she is, or believes herself to be, incapable of action of any kind. By being so sensitive to the scene or situation in which she finds herself, Fanny all but gives up any capacity for agency. Her passivity amounts to an unwillingness and then an inability to 'disturb the universe'. At Sotherton, when Fanny has overtired herself with walking, Edmund suggests that she has been too slow to speak up: '"Why would you not speak sooner?"' he asks and again, although it is a small incident, there is the hint given that extreme self-suppression, even if undertaken to spare others on one's behalf, is unnatural and can lead to the need for others to bother themselves to an excessive degree in caring for an invalid. In the play scene, when Fanny is asked to take a part, she does not say that she must not, nor that she may not, but rather she says, '"No, indeed, I cannot act."' She lacks histrionic ability certainly, but the phrase hints at a greater inability, and suggests that while she may be avoiding sins of commission she is not altogether free from sins of omission.

Fanny's inability to act with determination is exposed further in a scene with more telling implications for her character. When she refuses Henry Crawford's offer of marriage she is questioned closely by Sir Thomas and is unable to give him a satisfactory explanation of her conduct. He briefly suspects that her affections might be otherwise engaged, but dimisses the idea. Fanny fears further questioning: 'She would rather die than own the truth, and she hoped by a little reflection to fortify herself beyond betraying it.'[20] Fanny manages this situation very badly, but her motive again seems sound: she wishes to avoid having to confess her love for Sir Thomas's son, who has made no overture whatever. When questioned about Crawford's character however, she once again sacrifices principle and truth:

> 'Have you any reason, child, to think ill of Mr. Crawford's temper?'
> 'No, Sir!'

This is not in fact a direct lie, it is merely an equivocation, as the rest of the context makes clear:

> She longed to add, 'but of his principles I have'; but her heart sunk under the appalling prospect of discussion, explanation, and probably non-conviction. Her ill opinion of him was founded chiefly on observations, which, for her cousins' sake, she could scarcely dare mention to their father. Maria and Julia—and especially Maria, were so closely implicated in Mr. Crawford's misconduct, that she could not give his character, such as she believed it, without betraying them.[21]

Here, Fanny's principle of doing nothing to prejudice the interest of her cousins leads her once more into a contradictory situation. To preserve Maria and Julia she must displease and speak equivocally to their father. Although she knows the truth she lacks the distinctness and dramatic energy to affirm it. A strong denunciation of Crawford by Fanny might have inconvenienced Maria, but as it ironically turns out her refusal to speak—it is true she may not have been believed in any case—could be seen as contributing to Sir Thomas's further sufferance of Crawford and therefore contributing to the ultimate scandal when he runs off with Maria. Once again then, Fanny's inability to act, to play her part, seems to be something which does not escape her author's ironic notice.

But Fanny does develop, at least a little. She has shown a spirit responsive to the pleasures of drama and when she returns to Portsmouth, a visit intended by Sir Thomas to make her see the economic realities of her situation, she finds before her the active good sense of her sister Susan and she begins to benefit from the example. Susan in her own way is an improver at home:

> Susan saw that much was wrong at home, and wanted to set it right. That a girl of fourteen acting only on her own unassisted reason, should err in the method of reform was not wonderful; and Fanny soon became more disposed to admire the natural light of the mind which could so early distinguish justly, than to censure severely the faults of conduct to which it led. Susan was only acting on the same truths, and pursuing the same system, which her own judgment acknowledged, but which her more supine and yielding temper would have shrunk from asserting.[22]

Because Susan's manner is often wrong, Fanny takes upon herself what is called 'an office of authority' and she begins to give hints and suggestions to guide and inform her. Julia, Maria and Mary Crawford are insubstantial because they have surface manners only and little good nature; they are form without content. Susan, however, can benefit from education, because she has an inner sense which needs even more drawing out. This theme of education in the novel is not meant to be read as Jane Austen's urging of capitulation to society, but rather as her complex argument of the way in which culture is necessary and desirable. Culture, manner, is the ability to make social life an art rather than merely a fixed pattern of gestures. What is required is natural feeling actively cultivated and expressed.

This sense of active life is quite unlike Mrs Norris's 'spirit of activity' and to be able to 'act' one does seem to require some histrionic ability. Truth is not enough; it must be expressed dramatically. Merely to accept the current social fashion, as do Maria, Julia, Henry and Mary Crawford, is to allow oneself to be formed totally from without. It is simply to put on the costume that society offers. The type of acting that results may on occasion be effective, but it cannot be so for long. On the other hand, to pay no attention whatever to the custom and manners of those around one must lead to a kind of solipsism, perhaps like that of Mrs Norris or Lady Bertram, or perhaps that of Fanny herself. And the phrase used for Fanny's temper, 'supine and yielding', must indicate yet again where Jane Austen's sympathies lie and at what an ironic distance from Fanny they can be. To be yielding may on occasion be appropriate, but to be supine is to be incomplete as a person.

It seems then that one must beware of two complementary dangers: on the one hand hiding, disguising or killing off inner sense by donning a social mask or *persona*, and on the other hand donning none at all. A *persona* is obviously needed, in order to provide the dramatic medium which will allow inner truth to appear and act in public, but it needs somehow to be one's own *persona*. Fanny seems to be slowly awakening to this fact when she takes the momentous step of joining a circulating library on her own: 'She became a subscriber—amazed at being anything in *propria persona*, amazed at her own doings in every way; to be a renter, a chuser of books!'[23] Once one develops an ear for indulgent irony of course: it is impossible not to hear it comically present in that bathetic comment on Fanny's 'daring'.

There is a sense in which Austen presents a profound analysis of what one could call 'situational ethics'. The central principle is in fact one which does have some current appeal still, one would hope, and it is the realisation so well caught in that phrase of George Eliot's about Dorothea when she begins to discover that other people have 'equivalent centres of self'. In a passage describing Julia, who is forced to keep company with Mrs Rushworth and Mrs Norris rather than with any of the young men, Jane Austen comments:

> The politeness which she has been brought up to practise as a duty, made it impossible for her to escape; while the want of that higher species of self-command, that just consideration of others, that knowledge of her own heart, that principle of right which had not formed any essential part of her education, made her miserable under it.[24]

Here politeness and duty are, after all, only stand-ins in the absence of that inner light which is a 'just consideration of others', which is also love. Fanny repeats the idea in one of her censures of Henry when she says that he has no 'principle to supply as a duty what the heart was deficient in'.[25]

One can conclude that *Mansfield Park* is not simply a book about the need for propriety, in so far as propriety is passive obedience to a code of rules. Mrs Norris sets up as an active paragon of propriety, but she is never right and lapses into paralysis. If propriety enjoins passivity in young girls then the novel is an exposure of the inadequacy of mistaking such a rule for an ethic.[26] To be free, to act significantly and ethically, at least two things are required in the world of Jane Austen. One must, on the one hand, avoid the tyranny of the agent, and on the other the tyranny of the scene. In Kenneth Burke's phrase, what is needed is a proper 'scene–agent' ratio. It can be seen that *Mansfield Park* might be read as a playful inversion of *Emma* in which a too active imagination and temper make assumptions and arrangements which have nothing whatever to do with the requirements of the scene. For Emma's active imaginings to become significant in a world of other agents, she needs to develop a clearer perception of the independent reality of the scene. Fanny, on the contrary, lacks precisely what Emma is so richly endowed with. Fanny can see, she can sense, what every actor in the scene is conscious of, but she brings a spirit of activity barely adequate to the needs of the scene. If Emma's maturity is dependent on her toning down, then Fanny's requires a bit of highlighting, a bit of colour, a bit of action. Given this, it is no wonder that *Emma* is the more satisfying novel. Both books make essentially the same point and one is an ironic inversion of the other. If Emma's moral education seems to some a tedious interference on the part of Austen with the liveliness of her character, then *Mansfield Park* helps give us a fuller vision of Austen's intent. Fanny's morality is too boring, too lifeless, to be anything else than deserving of the ironic detachment with which it is treated.

It should be clear that *Mansfield Park*, while it does seem to argue for a coincidence of inner and outer, is not to be dismissed as merely a defence of sincerity or accepting one's place in society.[27] It is rather, and once again, an attempt to discover the way to free, significant, and ethical action in the world. To act significantly means, first of all, to act freely with full awareness of the scene in which one finds oneself. Impulsive, insensible action, proves insubstantial; it has no lasting meaning. By contrast, to let the definition of the scene provide one's meaning is to will oneself into vitiation of mind, paralysis and immorality. This can be expressed by a further shift from a dramatic metaphor to a linguistic one. One can live neither by clichés nor by neologisms. What is needed, borrowing a phrase this time from Owen Barfield, is an interaction of 'speaker's meaning' with 'lexical meaning'. Anne Elliot is relevant, whose 'word has no weight'. In *Persuasion* what is required is a change in scenic circumstances before Anne's word can be recognised as weighty, whereas what is required in *Mansfield Park* is greater energy of self-expression from Fanny. To act in *propria persona* means to discover oneself dramatically in action using language significantly, and the required drama is one that comes artfully between the two extremes of hypocrisy and solipsism. The story of the novel in the nineteenth century is not the story of the way in which characters accommodate themselves to society, nor of the way in which they take on definition in society.[28] It is a much more subtle and important story than that. It is the story of the way in which characters *achieve* definition and significance in society, although culture is a better word than society.[29] Fanny has the nature, but this nature has needed culture; it has lacked art. And once again, for Austen as for Pope, art is nature not naked nor raw, but dressed to advantage.

5 Agents and Patients in Dickens

As has often been remarked, perhaps most recently by Michael Goldberg in his *Carlyle and Dickens*,[1] Carlyle's influence on Dickens begins to make itself felt by the time of *Dombey and Son*. The earlier picaresque, comic Dickens never disappears, but he begins to direct his attention increasingly to social conditions and to find the source of evils in society, in the fact of society itself. What has perhaps not been so widely noticed is that Dickens' analysis of social institutions includes also an analysis of language; it is logical that the two should be treated together, since language is, at least up to a point, a social institution. *Hard Times*, which is an extension of many of the themes of *Dombey and Son*, contains a revelation of the ineffectuality of the 'blue-books' with their dead facts. These blue-books are referred to as the 'stutterings' of Parliament, and the metaphor makes us realise anew that social institutions, particularly that of Parliament, are language. In *Hard Times* Dickens also makes clear the hard logic that makes his attitude to social problems so often perplexing to the merely utilitarian, or to those 'hysterical women' described by Yeats who insist that something drastic must be done: If society is corrupt, then all its institutions are corrupt and therefore any attempt by social, or parliamentary means to correct social evils is doomed since the means are already tainted. If social institutions are to be changed, then what is required is a renewed language. How, though, does one overcome the paradox that language is social? Despite the more sombre Carlylean overtones of *Dombey and Son*, there is still reason for arguing that the novel is essentially an optimistic one in that it conceives of a way of overcoming both the problem of social institutions like those suggested by the firm of 'Dombey and Son' (in which a family relationship is corrupted into a commercial one) as well as any problems that inhere in the fact of language itself.

The title of the novel suggests the dual concern, in that it is ambiguous, and it is the ambiguity of language, or rather of signs, that is one of the central focuses of the book. The phrase 'Dombey and Son' is an ambiguous signifier, pointing either to the firm (the social economic institution), or to the personal, family relationship. The story deals with the evil that results from confusing the one 'signified' with the other. The villain of the piece is Carker and he works his evil by relying on the power inherent in ambiguity and misinterpretation. Although Carker dresses 'in imitation of the great man whom he served', he stops short of Mr Dombey's stiffness. This divergence in dress styles is in itself a sign of some sort, and indeed Carker is like a gloss on the main text: 'Some people quoted him indeed, in this respect, as a pointed commentary, and not a flattering one, on his icy patron—but the world is prone to misconstruction, and Mr Carker was not accountable for its bad propensity.'[2] Carker's evil is recognised in his perverted sense of agency. He claims for himself an innocence arising from passivity: he intends nothing, he arranges nothing. He blames 'society' and in a sense he is absolutely correct in doing so since, regarded from the social point of view, language does not communicate anything. It is a neutral and confusing array of possible signals.

The arbitrariness, the ambiguity of language and the need for interpretation, demand active participation on the part of the signaller. Carker's denial of intentional agency sets the machinery, the heartless machinery of society, free to work evil. Obviously this type of evildoing can turn on the perpetrator. Since he chooses to believe in a fiction of his own lack of agency, he in turn is potentially a victim of the confusing signals of the system of signs bereft of intent. Edith Dombey leads Carker to believe that she will pay him a 'voluptous compensation for past restraint'[3]—Carker economises even sexually, and the pathos of his delusion here almost humanises him—and she is able to fool him precisely because he has never worried about what lies behind words. He has worn the clothes of sincerity but he has never intended sincerity. Towards Mr Dombey he has a 'deeply conceived' and 'perfectly expressed' manner of subservience. He seems to say to him, '"Mr. Dombey, to a man in your position from a man in mine, there is no show of subservience compatible with the transaction of business between us, that I should think sufficient. . . ."' The narrative comment on this perfectly expressed attitude is interesting: 'If he had carried these words about with him printed on a placard, and had constantly offered it to Mr.Dombey's perusal on the breast of his coat, he could not have been more explicit than he was.'[4] Absolutely explicit, he has no time for anything merely implicit, such as good will.

When his brother John tries to suggest some sort of family reconciliation, because he fears his sister Harriet is suffering from the enforced estrangement, Carker the Manager quibbles about the choice of words. John, the Junior, says he is as sorry that Harriet has chosen to live with him and not the Manager as Carker the Manager is angry about it:

'Angry?' repeated the other, with a wide show of his teeth.
'Displeased. Whatever words you like best. You know my meaning. There is no offence in my intention.'[5]

It is Carker's insane refusal to read intentions, and his insistence on the letter (when the letter is arbitrary—'whatever words you like best'—) that lead to his emotional bankruptcy. His often mentioned teeth are obviously hypocritical in their smiling, and they suggest a carnivorous propensity on his part. Carker's cat-like dentition is like that of the Cheshire cat; all the rest of him could disappear because he is nothing but mouth. His messages are all formed on the surface, with no admixture of heart: 'Mr. Carker, with his mouth from ear to ear, repeated, 'Time enough.' Not articulating the words, but bowing his head affably, and forming them with his tongue and lips.'[6] Like the Cheshire cat, he is appearance but not reality. Take away the mouth and there would be nothing. In this instance the Cheshire cat will be defeated by the other cat, that of Dick Whittington, so often alluded to by Captain Cuttle with reference to Walter.

The thematic appeal to fairy-tale suggests that Dickens does not have a completely rational analysis of society and its evils, but does believe they can be overcome whatever their cause; he appeals, therefore, to the magic of the fairy-tale. The magical victory of good over evil, of Florence and Walter over Carker, is not entirely without its logic, however; it is not merely arbitrary nor wish-fulfilling. What Dickens is saying about Carker is something almost metaphysical; he is suggesting that Carker is insubstantial in his *being*. Carker is killed by a train, but it would be a mistake to consider the train sequences in detail to attempt to discover what Dickens is saying about the advent of this new machine. The train figures in the story because it was topical, and because it would serve as a device to get rid of Carker. And it is nothing more than a convenience. Carker must die because somehow he is a character lacking substance. The logic of his demise might be put another way. Since evil is evil, it can be recognised by the destructive effects it produces. Carker can cause pain and suffering, just as acid can eat away glass. If hydrochloric acid is being conveyed in a glass bottle, sooner or later the container itself will decay. Carker as an agent of a real but deleterious evil must, then, destroy himself. The train is a mere anticlimactic device. Carker has already been destroyed by Edith who beats him at his own game of ambiguity. It is precisely his relationship to and way of using language that indicate the disorientation and ultimate fragility of his personality. He forms his words with his lips and teeth; further, he has a 'voiceless manner'. Carker does not stand behind his words; more than that, he does not exist behind his words. Existence implies some kind of agency and Carker is not actively attempting to convey an inner reality; he is not attempting to encode any message, but is passively allowing the potential chaos of misinterpretation free rein.

The train that kills him does have some further significance beyond mere narrative necessity, however. It represents an energy, an activity almost cosmic in its proportions, that will sweep down and annihilate those who choose Carker's kind of passivity. Any doubt about whether the train is meant by Dickens to be a force for good or evil, can be clarified by considering that the train is after all a mere social tool, an institution of tracks and possible turnings and possible combinations of cars, very much like the network of language. The train, then, represents the vengeance that 'system' will take on those who abnegate their responsibility to be creative and active in their use of signs, or systems. Mr Toodle, the engineer, advises his son Rob the Grinder to avoid secrecy, and he uses the train metaphor:

> 'You see, my boys and gals,' said Mr. Toodle, looking round upon his family, 'wotever you're up to in a honest way, it's my opinion as you can't do better than be open. If you find yourselves in cuttings or in tunnels, don't you play no secret games. Keep your whistles going, and let's know where you are.'[7]

So Carker's death by train is important in suggesting that he dies because of a failure to signal.

One might think that it's not altogether that easy. If the world is open to misunderstanding, merely keeping signals going is likely to lead to yet more railway accidents, as it were, by multiplying the possibilities for misreading. The recognition that language itself can fail is a highly problematic one for the artist in words. One course open after such recognition is to shrug one's shoulders and lapse into silence, as some of Beckett's characters seem about to do. Another course is Hemingway's, keep language as close to the line of simple events as possible and avoid the rhetoric of sentiment. Yet another way is to believe that by creative effort and voluminous work the difficulty will be overcome. This latter seems to be Dickens' path, and Faulkner's later on is not too dissimilar. If Dickens' solution to social problems often seems magical, it is not unconsidered, and he is aware that the Toodle solution to the problems found in the 'junction a man's thoughts is' is not always enough. If life before the Fall were some kind of exultant, expressive state of constant Hosannah, the naive attempt to recreate an unfallen world in this day gives rise perhaps to tootles and not heavenly trumpets. The Pickwick solution of retreat into some Dingley Dell world safe from the terrible troubles of daily life seems no longer to have Dickens' full assent. Even the amiable Captain Cuttle, for all his virtues of the heart, does not escape his author's irritation, possibly at his irrelevancy. In Chapter 25, 'Strange News of Uncle Saul', the narrator interrupts the dramatic interchanges of the Captain and Rob the Grinder in order to summarise the situation more economically:

> Such, reduced into plain language, and condensed within a small compass, was the final result and substance of Captain Cuttle's deliberations: which took a long time to arrive at this pass, and were, like some more public deliberations, very discursive and disorderly.[9]

Given Dickens' attitude to Parliament, this is a very sharp comment indeed on Cuttle, earned because he represents too ready a solution to the problems about signalling that Dickens wants to pursue.

Dickens does not of course merely dismiss in irritation characters like Captain Cuttle and his often consulted oracle Bunsby. In a novel with the sea as a recurrent image, particularly with reference to Paul Dombey Jr, who hears the waves whispering some message to him which turns out to be the one word 'death', nautical and fishy names are of some importance. If the sea is death—and it is also merely silence; Toots we find on one occasion 'apparently drowned' at the bottom of 'a deep well of silence'[9]—then those with names like Cuttle, Gills and Morfin, obviously know how to swim in the destructive element. While Dickens suggests that Cuttle's vision is not altogether a full nor universally acceptable one, he is also at pains to suggest that it is infinitely preferable to other alternatives, that of Mrs Skewton or Major Bagstock for instance. The nearness to danger and delusion of Cuttle is suggested by his response to Carker. He has gone to Carker seeking some confirmation that 'Dombey and Son' intend some bright future for Walter, encompassing his eventual marriage to Florence. Carker equivocates throughout, but the Captain sees only what he wishes to see, being blind perhaps to mere surfaces:

> Mr. Carker still blandly assenting in the same voiceless manner, Captain Cuttle was strongly confirmed in his opinion that he was one of the most agreeable men he had ever met, and that even Mr. Dombey might improve himself on such a model.[10]

He parts with the hearty comment, '"I ain't a man of many words, but I take it very kind of you to be so friendly, and above-board."' The irony of the passage, of course, is at Carker's expense, and one cannot, perhaps, expect Cuttle to see through the subtleties of one such as Carker. It is important to note the point Dickens is making about Cuttle, though: it is exactly his relative innocence that makes him blind to evil when it stares him in the face. The narrator's comment is: 'The unconscious Captain walked out in a state of self-glorification that imparted quite a new cut to the broad blue suit.' The Captain's carelessness with words may be something that he and his kind can transcend, but it does not go unnoticed by Dickens.

The reason that Cuttle can transcend his own carelessness with signs is that Dickens believes that a loving, warm-hearted intention to communicate easily overcomes any difficulties occasioned by mere signifiers. *What* will be expressed is ultimately more important than the means of expression. The Captain will spend a Sunday afternoon smoking over a Bible without apparently reading anything, and he often adjures one to 'overhaul the Wollume' and make a note of the important passage, but there is little evidence that he himself actually overhauls many volumes. The reason for this is that he himself is a kind of walking library in potential. So far is he from the necessity of actually reading the Bible that he seems often on the point of composing an eccentric one of his own:

> 'Wal'r, my boy,' replied the Captain, 'in the Proverbs of Solomon you will

find the following words, "May we never want a friend in need, nor a bottle to give him!" When found, make a note of.'

Here the Captain stretched out his hand to Walter, with an air of downright good faith that spoke volumes; at the same time repeating (for he felt proud of the accuracy of his quotation), 'When found, make a note of.'[11]

With his odd notion of what makes public sense as a communication, with the wild and glittering array of meaningless signals sent out by his flashing hook, Cuttle, to the general public, must always remain a being 'mysterious and incomprehensible'. To a more personal public, one willing to read between his signs, his message is clear.

His oracle, John Bunsby, is possibly one more step down the road to incomprehensibility, but between Bunsby and Cuttle there is an intuitive understanding based on mutual feeling. When they consult together they are not exchanging pieces of encoded information; instead they are communing in some deep sense to discover if their virtually unconscious emotions coincide. If Cuttle can establish some mutual basis of feeling, he has something as good as an oracle—and far less ambiguous—on which to act. On one occasion on which 'Solemn reference is made to Mr. Bunsby', his audience waits in awe before the 'profound authority', to be rewarded with the following:

After sundry failures to put his arm around Miss Nipper in this wise, the Commander, addressing himself to nobody, thus spake; or rather the voice within him said of its own accord, and quite independent of himself, as if he were possessed by a gruff spirit:

'My name's Jack Bunsby!'

The Captain provides a gloss meant to be enlightening: '"He was christened John," cried the delighted Captain Cuttle. "Hear him!"' The Captain's glee at this oracular pronouncement is only heightened by what follows from Bunsby: '"Whereby," proceeded the voice, "why not? If so, what odds? Can any man say otherwise? No. Awast then!"'[12] Now, the Captain is able to make sense out of such a communication and its continuation, which would be too lengthy to quote. In fact, the most important part of the message is just possibly the simple, or exclamatory, announcement of his name. Being able to say that much, he at least provides evidence that he is there: I can say my name, therefore I am. Compared with Carker, Bunsby has undoubted substantiality of being. It is interesting to note that Bunsby, like Carker, is passive. He does not speak, but a voice within him does. The difference is that the hollow Carker is in fact only wilful, while Bunsby's fullness with inner being overcomes the confusion of surface signals. There is a sense in which Bunsby has so much interior being, or content, that, because it cannot fail to make itself known, it matters little what particular form of expression is used. The appearance in the form of a visible sign, could not possibly convey all that Bunsby, or Cuttle, is inside; so a mere name, or a wave of a hook, will do as well as any other sign. The surface sign is merely a clue to the reality; it points to it but does not completely contain it. Some minimal sign, such as a name or a wave, is necessary, however, if only to give one something specific to look beyond. This seems to be the point of the Captain's earlier comment to Walter, who has asked for the name of the Captain's friend: ' "His name's Bunsby," said the Captain. "But Lord, it might be anything for the matter of that, with such a mind as his!" '[13]

In contrast to Cuttle and Bunsby, who overcome problems of mediation by means of heart and good intentions, Mrs Skewton massacres the language—and it occasionally fights back. Her vague grasp both on language and on the reality it points to is suggested by her often repeated phrase 'what's-his-name'. She says of her relationship with her daughter Edith: 'there is a what's-his-name—a gulf—opened between us.'[14] When what's-his-names are as deep as gulfs, one wants wary walking. Not only the depths below are dismissed, so are promises of beatification above. Mrs Skewton says, ' "But seclusion and contemplation are my what's-his-name—" ', to which Edith replies, ' "If you mean Paradise, Mama, you had better say so, to render yourself intelligible. . ." '.[5] Just as Mr Podsnap can dismiss everything not English, Mrs Skewton plays fast and loose with the nomenclature of non-English religions: ' "My dearest Edith, there is such an obvious destiny in it, that really one might almost be induced to cross one's arms upon one's frock, and say, like those wicked Turks, there is no What's-his-name but Thingummy, and What-you-may-call-it is his prophet!" '[16] The capital W perhaps denotes respect, but the indication is that even a properly English God would find that this Cleopatra of Society would have forgotten His name should He turn up for dinner some day. This carelessness about articulacy finally takes its toll, when Mrs Skewton lies dying and her speech begins more accurately to reflect the spiritual insubstantiality of the speaker. She cannot recall at all the name of her pretended lover Major Bagstock, and she refers to Dombey indifferently as either 'Grangeby' or 'Domber': ' "Now, my dearest Grangeby," said Mrs Skewton, "you must posively prom," she cut some of her words short, and cut out others altogether, "come down very soon." '[17]

Like Mrs Norris of *Mansfield Park*, Mrs Skewton has been characterised by a spirit of activity, but it has been an insubstantial and mechanical activity which gives way ultimately to paralysis: ' "I won't have vistors—really don't want vistors," she said; "little repose—and all that sort of thing—is what I quire. No odious brutes must proach me till I've shaken off this numbness . . ." '.[18] When Cuttle's syntax breaks down it does not matter since there is so much of him inside that what he intends easily leaps over gulfs of mediation. Mrs Skewton, on the other hand, has had no inner resources at all. Like Carker (and the later Mrs General of *Little Dorrit*) her energy has been exercised mechanically, only on the surface, the social surface of life. Language, of course, is not only a malign, inert, or neutral vehicle, however much it may seem to be so at times. It can also tell the truth, even amidst, or by means of, ambiguity. Mrs Skewton describes her love of Nature, her passion for cows, and outlines what she desires, or wants, or lacks:

> 'What I want,' drawled Mrs. Skewton, pinching her shrivelled throat, 'is heart.' It was frightfully true in one sense, if not in that in which she used the phrase. 'What I want, is frankness, confidence, less conventionality, and freer play of soul. We are so dreadfully artificial.'
> We were, indeed.[19]

The broken speech and the shrivelled throat, point to what it is destroys Mrs Skewton. She has no heart, and she does not actively attempt to communicate heart by means of language.

We are not surprised to hear that Captain Cuttle has a 'heart of oak' which differentiates him from the Skewtons of the world, but it is perhaps a little unusual to be told that he is wood all the way through: 'The Captain was one of those timber-looking men, suits of oak as well as hearts, whom it is almost impossible for the liveliest imagination to separate from any part of their dress, however insignificant.'[20] In this metaphorical sense, the Captain really does wear his heart on his sleeve. There is no gulf between his surface appearance and his depth; the clothes reveal him fully. The comment is often made of Dickens' 'grotesques', or of his 'caricatures', that they are mere bundles of wooden gestures without inner meaning; that they are cramped into their shapes by the Procrustean bed of Victorian society that allows little free play of personality. It would seem that such a comment is completely unacceptable. Cuttle can be described by constant reference to his glazed hat, or his clothing, because for Dickens this character is one who appears fully despite what particular part of his surface is referred to. Cuttle can afford to be grotesque, or incomplete on the surface, because his task in the novel is to show how innerness can dominate misleading surface representation. Also, Cuttle belongs to that magic world of fairy-tale, in which there is no gulf of mediation. So he is wooden throughout, in the sense that his metaphorical heart of oak rises to the surface and transforms his whole self. Such a complex and perhaps repetitive comment on Cuttle is needed in order to be able to see what Dickens is suggesting when he uses a similar 'wooden' metaphor for Dombey, who is at one point described as 'laying himself on a sofa like a man of wood, without a hinge or a joint in him'.[21]

Because of the metaphor used for these two characters, one is led to suspect that Dickens somehow associates Dombey and Cuttle in his mind. We have already noted that Cuttle does not altogether escape Dickens' irritation, and he is indeed suggesting that both these characters are not

fully human, that they are 'wooden' in that sense. He carefully differentiates Cuttle from Dombey, however, in the way hinted above. Cuttle
can be wooden on the surface, because it does not much matter with a heart
such as his. The direction is right for Cuttle: from inner to outer. Dombey is
another matter. He is not moved from within, but like a wooden man, or a
badly made and poorly jointed puppet, he is moved from without. The
forces of society, of money, pull the strings. Dombey, then, is the greater
Carker, in that he seems to have given up all vital, or inner, agency to the
external forces of society. It is now possible to see that Dickens is making an
extremely fine discrimination, by noting that, while both Carker and Dombey are passive, they remain extremely wilful and busy in the public world.
To be passive, then, does not necessarily mean having given up all motion.
It means to have given up the responsibility for one's own moving, directed
from within. The difference is suggested by the pun hidden in the word
'agent'—the pun which is at the heart of Conrad's *The Secret Agent*. In the
first sense, to be an agent is to be free to act on one's own behalf. It is to be
human. In the second sense, one can be an agent by conducting someone
else's business for him; the secret of success here is to have no inner
promptings of one's own, but to be completely directed by one's master, or
employer. To be an agent in the second sense is directly contrary to the
possibility of being an agent in the first sense. When Dickens' novels urge
us to activity, to agency, they direct our attention first to the dangers
inherent in the ambiguous word, then carefully lead us to prefer the
primary sense.

    Dombey, Carker and Cuttle need to be considered together in this way, in
order to see how carefully Dickens notes their similarities as well as their
differences. There is one remaining distinction to be made, and it is that
between Dombey and Carker, both apparently agents in the second sense.
Carker seems always to have been a hollow man and so it is unlikely that he
can ever make up his deficiency of being. He must be destroyed. Dombey,
however, has also had a home life. If he has not contributed much to it, at
least he has been exposed to the potentially benign influences of his situation. He has been loved by Florence and it seems reasonable to say that he
has loved Paul, although this love is perhaps inextricably mixed with
egoism and ambition. If he is at one point a man of wood, and at another a
'frozen gentleman'[22] the mixed metaphors perhaps suggest that he can be
kindled and thaw himself out. Indeed, it seems that Dombey is not to be
thought to have no interior, like Carker. He has had innerness, but has
repressed himself. He has attempted to live only on the surface and to put
an impassable gulf between depth and surface; not with complete success,
however, because of the overwhelming power of the inner world, if it exists
at all. If there is any inner self, it seems that it must make some external
signals of its presence:

Though he hide the world within him from the world without—which he believes has but one purpose for the time, and that, to watch him eagerly wherever he goes—he cannot hide those rebel traces of it, which escape in hollow eyes and cheeks, a haggard forehead, and a moody, brooding air. Impenetrable as before, he is still an altered man; and, proud as ever, he is humbled, or those marks would not be there.[23]

The passage refers to Dombey's condition on discovering that Edith has run off with Carker, but the phrase suggests what has been his characteristic habit; he has been hiding the inner world from the world without. As he watches Florence playing merrily with the new baby, Paul, the narrator says of him, 'Was Mr. Dombey pleased to see this? He testified no pleasure by the relaxation of a nerve; but outward tokens of any kind of feeling were unusual with him.'[29] It is to be expected, then, that his moral recovery is a possibility if the expressive connection can once again be made for him. Dombey has been capable of emotion, but, like Sir Thomas Bertram in *Mansfield Park*, he has bottled it up and repressed all external signs of his internal world.

Having now pursued a different line of investigation around to the same point, one might be willing to conclude that the naive expressiveness of Cuttle is, after all, Dickens' ideal and his message to the world. The gloriously shining face of Cuttle is hard to ignore:

> But never in all his life had the Captain's face so shone and glistened, as when, at last, he sat stationary at the tea-board, looking from Florence to Walter, and from Walter to Florence. Nor was this effect produced or at all heightened by the immense quantity of polishing he had administered to his face with his coat-sleeve during the last half-hour. It was solely the effect of his internal emotions. There was a glory and delight within the Captain that spread itself over his whole visage, and made a perfect illumination there.[25]

The excess of joy and glory in this sort of passage is perhaps what leads many modern readers to nod sagely and say dismissively, 'Sentiment. Victorian sentiment.' It would make much more sense for us to say wish-fulfilment, however. The excess of the passage arises, more likely, from Dickens' worried insistence that life *must* be like this, it *ought* to be. His belief that a perfect state of expressivity, in which the inner world is directly conveyed to the outer world, does not last long. He has constantly in mind the troubling notion that emotions are mediated when they are expressed. The mere possibility of hypocrisy gives rise to constant and careful reconsiderations of his ideas. It is possible that one might be able to counterfeit Cuttle's signs of emotion without feeling his emotion. Equally it might be possible to be a person at least the emotional equal of Cuttle and yet be deprived of the conditions which allow full expression—indeed in which expression of emotion would only lead to its destruction rather than its

completion. Problems such as these come to a focus with the characters of
Edith and Florence Dombey.

Having considered only Dombey and Cuttle one could come to the
mistaken (because over-simple) conclusion that Dickens' 'philosophy' consists of a detestation of repression of emotion, and of hypocrisy (both
examples of the misuse of signifiers). One comment about the character
of Florence must make us revise any over-simple notions we might have
about Dickens' purpose. When she is captured by Mrs Brown several
things work together to enable Florence to tell Mrs Brown about herself:

> The old woman's threats and promises; the dread of giving her offence;
> and the habit, unusual to a child, but almost natural to Florence now, of
> *being quiet, and repressing what she felt, and feared, and hoped*; enabled her to
> do this bidding, and to tell her little history. . . [26]

With Florence, so obviously the centre of values of the novel, we can see
that the 'tootles' philosophy of 'keep your whistles going' is just not sufficient. While on one level Dickens wants to believe that being active and
expressive is good, he knows that to be active requires a setting. And it is
just possible that the setting might enforce passivity and that passivity so
enforced, or the repression of signs or whistles, is not an indication of moral
insubstantiality.

The reason Florence can break the circuit connecting the inside and
outside with impunity is that her motives are benign: she wishes to convince her father that she has always loved him and she hopes this knowledge of love will bring about a change in him. To keep her whistles going
would further alienate her father from her and, as she realises, the world
would take her part and the father she loves would suffer needlessly (in her
estimation). All this is made plain in the scene at Sir Barnet Skettles',
after Paul's death, when Florence has been overhearing herself described as
poorer than an orphan because outcast from a living parent's love. She
makes a resolution to repress all signs of her distress:

> Meantime she must be careful in no thoughtless word, or look, or burst of
> feeling awakened by any chance circumstance, to complain against him,
> or to give occasion for these whispers to his prejudice.
>
> Even in the response she made the orphan child, to whom she was
> attracted strongly, and whom she had such occasion to remember, Flor-
> ence was mindful of him. If she singled her out too plainly (Florence
> thought) from among the rest, she would confirm—in one mind cer-
> tainly: perhaps more—the belief that he was cruel and unnatural. Her
> own delight was no set-off to this. What she had overheard was a reason,
> not for soothing herself, but for saving him; and Florence did it, in
> pursuance of the study of her heart. [27]

Before concluding what is obviously the case, that Florence, being a saint of sorts, is the exception that proves the rule about expressivity, one should note closely just what she is doing. She is deliberately deceiving the world at large, or is trying to—without much success—into the belief that her father is not cruel and unnatural; and she hopes to achieve this by means of a complete repression of all natural signs of her feelings. But of course, Florence is a saint of sorts. She is one more example of a recurrent joke of Dickens'; she is a benign hypocrite, barely even letting her right hand know what her left hand doeth. Because her motives are good, she can indulge in the alteration of appearances, or in the creation of fictions. This is obviously an important theme in a work which is itself an appearance, or fiction.

Edith, when she is closely associated with Florence can, indeed must, indulge in the alteration of appearances. Dombey feels threatened by the comparison the public will make when they see the easy affection that grows between Florence and her step-mother, Edith. Under the influence of Carker, Dombey insists that there be no further intimacy between the pair, threatening some misfortune to Florence should his wishes not be met. After some time Florence speaks to Edith about the new and strange coldness between them and Edith explains that they must be somewhat estranged: ' "Not wholly estranged. Partially: and only that, in appearance, Florence, for in my own breast I am still the same to you, and ever will be. But what I do is not done for myself." '[28] As Florence had identified her-self with her father, so Edith, by means of sympathetic imagination, sets Florence's lot before her own, going so far as to interfere with the natural expression of emotion. As the narrative suggests, however, occasionally such unnaturalness in the matter of signals is natural:

> Was Mr. Dombey's master-vice, that ruled him so inexorably, an unnatural characteristic? It might be worthwhile, sometimes, to in-quire what Nature is, and how men work to change her, and whether, in the enforced distortions so produced, it is not natural to be un-natural.[29]

The unnatural interference with the use of signs and appearances that Edith and Florence are driven to is justifiable only in special circumstances, however. The manipulation of signs must be benign: that is, it must be intended for some selfless end and therefore must be freely and actively undertaken in order to achieve this end—it is important to note that Edith must *actively* do what she is *driven* to do by Dombey. For her to continue to express her feeling for Florence would be passively to acquiesce to 'nature' and would end in suffering for Florence. Further, manipulation of surface signs is only justified when the inner message is positive: 'in my own breast I am still the same to you'.

Under the influence of Florence, Edith becomes capable of love and selfless action. It has not always been thus with her, nor does the state continue long. She has been so alienated from her deepest self by her mother's offering of her (prostituting her) in the marriage market, that even her own body no longer serves to express her own will. Her very beauty seems an instrument beyond her will, that keeps signalling to the public a message—'I am for sale', for instance—that she would deny:

> It was a remarkable characteristic of this lady's beauty that it appeared to vaunt and assert itself without her aid, and against her will. She knew that she was beautiful: it was impossible that it could be otherwise: but she seemed with her own pride to defy her very self.[30]

This split between what the world sees and what Edith wills leads to a mistaken passivity on Edith's part, that makes her for a while very akin to Carker. She believes that if she takes no active part at all in her 'sale' to Dombey she will not be culpable if the results are not all good:

> Who takes me, refuse that I am . . . shall take me as this man does, with no art of mine put forth to lure him. He sees me at the auction, and he thinks it well to buy me. Let him! When he came to view me—perhaps to bid—he required to see the roll of my accomplishments. I gave it to him. When he would have me show one of them to justify his purchase to his men, I require of him to say which he demands, and I exhibit it. I will do no more. He makes the purchase of his own will . . . and I hope it may never disappoint him. *I* have not vaunted and pressed the bargain . . .'[31]

Just as Carker does, Edith here is leaving the world free to make its own misconstructions of ambiguous signs. Under Florence's loving influence, however, she becomes once again active, refusing to be a mere exhibit:

> 'I will hold no place in your house to-morrow, or on any recurrence of to-morrow. I will be exhibited to no one, as the refractory slave you purchased, such a time. If I kept my marriage-day, I would keep it as a day of shame. Self-respect! appearances before the world! what are these to me?'[32]

As an exhibit, Edith's body has been nothing more than a passive sign perverted from its proper end: that of revealing inner substance. Her appearance has been bought and is used by Dombey to suggest falsely to the world something about *his* inner being. This passive use of her appearance as an exhibit, or perverted sign, fits the pattern discussed earlier of the hollow sign. Edith makes a judgement on her life, one not dissimilar to that of Kurtz in *Heart of Darkness* in that it testifies to a similar moral courage: ' "I stand alone in the world, remembering well what a hollow world it has been to me, and what a hollow part of it I have been myself." '[33] The character of Edith is Dickens' way of proving that signs can be perverted, that whistles kept going can be hollow. The uncertainty that runs through his perception of the world and through his novels derives from just this apparently simple realisation of the potentially misleading nature of signs, and the human need to be realised in signs. Florence's ability to create a fiction, which is also, in a sense, a perversion of the normal signifying function of signs, testifies to Dickens' belief that despite the enormous philosophical difficulties in the matter, people can make themselves understood. What is required is not a lapse into silence, but faith that ultimately intention will make even fictions, with their complexly mediated messages, stand revealed.

Edith, believing the world to be hollow, and herself to be beyond saving, makes a mistake. She gives up completely on the world of appearances. She is certainly right in refusing to be Dombey's exhibit, but she goes too far when she refuses to appear at all, except under false signs. Having apparently left Dombey for Carker, Edith doubles her vengeance by refusing to pay Carker his dividend of voluptuous satisfaction and dismisses him. Edith, however, refuses to make it plain to the world that she has not had any illicit affair with Carker. The marked phrasing Dickens uses to convey Edith's resolution points directly to his central concern with the importance of signs. Edith explains her plan to the shocked Carker:

'I have resolved to bear the shame that will attach to me—resolved to know that it attaches falsely—that you know it too—and that he does not, never can, and never shall. I'll die, and make no sign.'[34]

Towards the end of the novel, Florence seeks out Edith and offers to try to win her father's forgiveness for her. Edith, under the influence of Florence, can no longer maintain her perverse silence and breaks out in intense speech: '"Florence!" she cried. "My better angel! Before I am mad again, before my stubbornness comes back and strikes me dumb, believe me, upon my soul I am innocent!"'[35] Edith's repression of signs, while it might seem superficially to be like Florence's earlier in the story, is quite different. The misuse of signs here is for a bad end, and it interferes with the expression of Edith's real feeling for Florence. It is therefore a bad fiction and we begin to see that the complexity and length of Dickens' analysis is in large part motivated by his need to consider carefully and from all sides the thorny problem of the morality of fiction—a topic, it should be noted, that we still too often believe to be the prerogative of twentieth-century writers. It is perhaps time to recognise that it is an inherent topic for any serious writer willing to face the necessary questions about his own use of fictional language.

Before leaving *Dombey and Son* it must be made clear that the subject of signs and fictions, and the conditions which must be met for a fiction to be justifiable, are really quite deliberate themes of the novel. It has already been seen that in a particular sense both Edith and Florence indulge in a special use of signs that can be called 'fiction'. Major Bagstock we discover maintains an interest in Miss Tox—until Mrs Skewton becomes a better object. It is not that he loves Miss Tox; it is rather that she is worthy of being thought infatuated with him. Major Bagstock 'was mightily proud of awakening an interest in Miss Tox, and tickled his vanity with the fiction that she was a splendid woman who had her eye on him'.[36] Miss Tox, of course, has her own little fiction that she might some day be thought worthy of becoming another Mrs Dombey. Captain Cuttle sets to work under the influence of a 'good natured delusion' to have a bit of a chat with Dombey and set Walter's future on the right tack. He has been so immersed in writing his own scenario of Walter's life that he finds it difficult to adjust himself to mere facts:

> He had arranged the future life and adventures of Walter so very dif-
> ferently, and so entirely to his own satisfaction; he had felicitated himself
> so often on the sagacity and foresight displayed in that arrangement, and
> had found it so complete and perfect in all its parts; that to suffer it to go to
> pieces all at once, and even to assist in breaking it up, required a great
> effort of his resolution.[37]

It might seem here that the Captain's fiction-making powers have cut him off completely from reality and trapped him in his own selfish schemes. The joke, of course, is that the sort of fictions that are entirely to Cuttle's satisfaction are those which breed most satisfaction for his friends and loved ones. Such delusions are not dangerous because they are created from love, and not a desire to mislead. Indeed Cuttle is seen at the close of the story having turned business itself into a fiction. Sol Gills has begun to find that his stock is turning itself over with remarkable regularity and 'As to his partner, Captain Cuttle, there is a fiction of a business in the Captain's mind which is better than any reality.'[38] Dickens' point may well be that it is only when business is recognised to be a fiction that it is properly conceived. Dombey has allowed himself to forget the fanciful and loving attitude that ought to go into a business and has turned a fiction into a nightmare.

Young Paul Dombey has an unusual ability to discriminate proper fic-
tions from improper ones. Mrs Pipchin, stung by Paul's sharp questions and truthful observations—he had been noticing how old she must be and how she eats all the mutton-chops and toast—advises him to remember '"the story of the little boy that was gored to death by a mad bull for asking questions"'. Paul's response, one can imagine, is typical of the way in which Dickens' mind responds to stories: with a strong sense of probabilities and possibilities of truth. '"If the bull was mad," said Paul, "how did *he* know that the boy had asked questions? Nobody can go and whisper secrets to a mad bull. I don't believe that story."'[39] The amazed Mrs Pipchin can only conclude that the unbelieving Paul is an Infidel.

Paul gives an important clue about the suspicious attitude Dickens himself can take towards fictions.

When Walter has been thinking of going to sea, his uncle Sol warns him off romantic dreaming: '"As to the Sea," he pursued, "that's well enough in fiction, Wally, but it won't do in fact: it won't do at all."'[40] In order to appreciate the dramatic irony of this comment it would be necessary to quote very lengthily from the scene in which it occurs. Briefly, Sol and Walter, having agreed to dismiss both fiction and the Sea, go on to develop an exciting fiction of adventure at sea; the story serves obviously as an often repeated ritual in their lives whereby they commune and rediscover the values they share. After the indulgence, Sol seems to come to himself upon recognising the inconsistency between his precept and his behaviour: '"The truth was, that the simple-minded Uncle in his secret attraction towards the marvellous and adventurous . . . had greatly encouraged the same attraction in the nephew . . ."'. The final narrative comment on this might well be meant to apply to Dickens' own novel, written to warn the unsuspecting of the dangers of fiction itself: 'It would seem as if there never was a book written, or a story told, expressly with the object of keeping boys on shore, which did not lure and charm them to the ocean, as a matter of course.'[41] Walter, with this proper 'improper' education of the heart and the imagination is, it is not surprising to find, 'what you may call a out'ard and visible sign of an in'ard and spirited grasp, and when found make a note of'.[42]

Cuttle's phrase indicates clearly that it is the problematical duality of outward sign and inward reality that catches Dickens' attention. If there is the danger of a lack of fit between inner and outer because of the arbitrary nature of signs themselves, one might expect that deliberately to make fictions is to give the screw that binds truth one more excruciating turn. It is Dickens' courage of imagination that makes him see that in this case two wrongs do add up to one right. If it is morally undesirable to be a hypocritical manipulator of signs, the solution to one's problems is not to give up on signs, but to recognise that by twisting them a bit more one can often, by means of fiction and fancy, let truth free. Dickens' attitude to language, or signs, is then paradoxical—although one might be led to conclude that it is merely confused. He believes in the necessity for signs, but he also shows an occasional contempt for them. It is in fact the Grinder system of schooling that seems to focus most on the machinery of language. Young students 'knew no rest from the pursuit of stony-hearted verbs, savage noun-substantives, inflexible syntactic passages. . . .' Before long they are convinced that 'all the fancies of the poets, and lessons of the sages, were a mere collection of words and grammar, and had no other meaning in the world'.[43] Miss Blimber, we learn, works in the graveyard of dead languages.[44] Florence, by contrast, is seen at one point 'relaxing in that dream within the dream which no tongue can relate'.[45] Although no tongue can relate it, it is precisely the artist's task to make it relatable.

Language is a kind of inevitable and necessary clothing for thought and one of the most important things to learn in the world is how to read. Language cannot, it seems, contain its message or imaginative or spiritual content, iconically. It serves only to point beyond itself to a transcending reality which must be seized by the imagination itself. To put it another way, truth, or an emotional or spiritual state, is in a sense general, extended and indivisible, while language is particular and analytical. It might seem as if the clothes can never be made to fit, but they must. It is possible to return to our starting place and say once again that Dickens in *Dombey and Son* shows the influence of Carlyle, but now one can conclude that it is not a new seriousness about society that Dickens gets from Carlyle, but rather a new metaphor about the nature of language as clothing, and the novel pursues the possibilities of this metaphor. As a recurrent image, of course, clothing plays an obvious part in the novel. One is never allowed to forget Cuttle's glazed hat. The first question put to young Paul Dombey by Mr Toots is '"Who's your tailor?"'[46] Mrs Brown kidnaps Florence apparently in order to steal her clothes and then dresses her in rags and 'the crushed remains of a bonnet that had probably been picked up from some ditch or dunghill'. Florence is redressed at home 'with great care, in proper clothes; and presently led . . . forth, as like a Dombey as her natural disqualifications admitted of her being made'.[47] The point, of course, is that Dombeyism is a kind of suit of clothes that can be put on, but if the inner self is active the clothes cannot really sink in and change the good heart. Once the heart is repressed, though, the clothing acts like Nessus' shirt and burns its way inward. Carker is 'always closely buttoned up and tightly dressed' and, as noted earlier, carries a message on his waistcoat. There is reference made to realities beyond mere clothing, such as Death, and a fashion that is very old, having come in 'with our first garments'.[48] Paul is the old-fashioned individual who can see through false clothing, like the stories of Mrs Pipchin. His insight apparently comes from his knowledge of what cannot be denied, mortality. This theme is developed throughout the rest of Dickens' novels and reaches a culmination in *Our Mutual Friend* which is about the need for a descent into a kind of death before a rebirth. The images of clothing in *Dombey and Son* reach a culmination in the goodhearted mutterings of Mr Toots:

'Captain Gills,' said Mr. Toots, 'my mind is greatly relieved. I wish to preserve the good opinion of all here. I—I—mean well, upon my honour, however badly I may show it. You know,' said Mr. Toots, 'it's exactly as if Burgess and Co. wished to oblige a customer with a most extraordinary pair of trousers, and *could not* cut out what they had in their minds.'[49]

It is worth recalling briefly some of the comments on symbols from *Sartor Resartus*,[50] in particular the dictum that 'Fantasy [is] the organ of the Godlike' and 'Man thereby, though based, to all seeming on the small Visible, does nevertheless extend down into the infinite deeps of the Invisible, of which Invisible, indeed, his Life is properly the bodying forth.' Teufels-drockh waxes enthusiastic on the delights of secrecy, delightful because secrecy leads ultimately to a greater revelation—and it is possible to see here how Dickens conceives of Florence's secrecy. It is just possible, however, that Dickens has one other source in mind that makes his view of the clothing of language that much more perplexing than that of Teufelsdrockh, and that source is St Paul's saying that here below we see as through a glass darkly (the phrase is used with reference to Eugene Wrayburn in *Our Mutual Friend*). Since this is so in normal circumstances, it takes a firm belief in fantasy to be able to continue to believe that a further darkening of the glass by means of writing fiction will in fact reveal truth. If the average sentient human being, like Mr Toots, finds that the trousers of his language do not always fit what is in his mind and heart, it is up to the artist to cut the clothes more exactly. He must show how one can fill the shapes, clothes or words, from inside and avoid above all else the dangers of hollowness. In terms of language, dead metaphors must be revivified by insight, clichés must be avoided. If worn-out symbols are not superannuated, as Teufels-drockh says, they threaten to '"hoodwink, to halter, to tether you; nay, if you shake them not aside, [threaten] to accumulate, and perhaps produce suffocation . . ."'. Institutions of business are also a kind of clothing, or language. And worn-out clothes such as the firm of Dombey and Son must be superannuated, to be replaced by the new firm of Sol Gills at the end of the novel. It can be seen that Dickens does, contrary to what his critics often say, offer what he conceives to be the solution of society's ills: learn how to wear clothes. If intention, heart, fantasy, can overcome the dangers inherent in language itself, then, on the clothes analogy, since institutions are merely another possible clothing for the human spirit, all that is needed to reform the evils of society is some change within. Clothes, businesses, language, all sign systems are like the sabbath in that they were made for man and not man for them.

To turn to *Little Dorrit* is to encounter the Circumlocution Office and be forcibly reminded that for Dickens a disorder in society is conceived of primarily as a linguistic disorder. On a personal level as well, a dis-orientation of personality is signalled by a disruption of syntax and meaning. By the time he has reached this novel, Dickens has less and less sympathy for the kinds of solutions offered by Captain Cuttle. The humour could never disappear, but some of the silliness did as he began to take his own discoveries about the nature of the world and the meaning of being an artist in words more seriously. With the theme of language and signs comes once again an urging to activity, particularly expressive activity. The evil of Mrs Clennam is precisely her secrecy, her suppression of the 'will' (and surely Dickens intends the pun), which is ended briefly by the loving agency of Little Dorrit. The rejected title 'Nobody's Fault' is clearly an indicator that one motive of the novel is to urge people to take individual

action and responsibility. The course of the narrative follows the resigned
Arthur Clennam into a new world of agency; he must learn to recover his
will. Any attempt to be an agent, however, entails learning also when to be
a patient. Dickens seems more and more convinced that the world will
never be much different; most men will always see as through a glass
darkly. Because it won't change, one must learn a kind of passivity in face of
the inevitable. Clennam, against the advice of his partner Doyce, tries to
take on the Circumlocution Office. Doyce argues that it is a mistake to waste
one's powers on such a monolith. Implicit in Doyce's and Dickens' attitude
is the assumption about evil that we found at work with Carker. If evil is left
alone it must eventually grind itself out—providing individuals are beginning to educate themselves out of the patterns of evil: will-lessness and
circumlocution. Little Dorrit herself provides the focus of the paradox that is
Dickens' conception of agency and passivity combined. Her life is one of
'active resignation',[51] a phrase ambiguous enough, but suggesting at least
that one must actively choose to resign oneself to one's lot and, further, that
once having accepted one's lot, one must continue to be active and working.
Clennam learns from Little Dorrit the difference between passive and active
resignation.

Still with the Great Exhibition of 1851 in mind, Dickens conceives of
society as merely external: 'in the great social Exhibition, accessories are
often accepted in lieu of the internal character.'[52] Once again mere external
signs, detached from and not generated by any inner resource, provide
Dickens a focus. And once again the acceptance of 'character' from outside
oneself is closely associated with corrupt language. Mrs Merdle, the paragon of the Exhibition Society, complains languidly of the trouble that her
eminence in Society brings her, and wishes that '"Society was not so
arbitrary, I wish it was not so exacting. . ."'. At this point she is interrupted
by her pet parrot: 'The parrot had given a most piercing shriek, as if its name
were Society and it asserted its right to its exactions.' The parroting that is
society is referred to again later in the novel when Mrs General insists that
no one have an opinion of his own and that everyone use the proper guide
book to discover what ought to be thought of Italy. Mrs Merdle continues
her mock complaint: '"We know it is hollow and conventional and worldly
and very shocking, but unless we are Savages in the Tropical Seas . . . we
must consult it. It is the common lot."'[53] This, one might argue, is another
version of active resignation. It is not really agency in the prime sense,
however. It is instead that sort of passivity, like Carker's, which sets the
destructive motions of the mechanism of Society to work. When hollow
language and mere convention are taken for real substance, absolute evil
springs up. The melodramatic villain Blandois, or Rigaud—whose name
might be anything it seems—appears quite plainly as the devil and, it turns
out, has no use for language at all. To Signor Panco he says, '"Words, sir,
never influence the course of the cards, or the course of the dice. Do you
know that? You do? I also play a game, and words are without power over

it."'[54] Typically, he claims that he is 'always a gentleman'. It is the 'gentleman', the member of the Exhibition who cares nothing for words, who seems capable of the most evil. Blandois, though, is another one of those characters who symbolically represent absolute evil and so carry the subject of language almost beyond the human realm. Such figures, according to the fortunate logic of Dickens' imagination, destroy themselves. Ultimately it is the game played within the boundaries of language that really concerns Dickens.

Blandois, as metaphysical a force of evil as he may at times seem, has a tawdry enough motive. He has 'a commodity to sell' to Mrs Clennam. As in most of Dickens' later novels the real villain is Moloch, and the evils associated with money manifest themselves as a denial of language. Ultimately the denial of language turns out to be a denial of human being, or, to put it another way, it is a form of suicide. Little Dorrit's brother Tip loses both articulacy and agency because of money:

> Here was her brother, a weak, proud, tipsy, young old man, shaking from head to foot, talking as indistinctly as if some of the money he plumed himself upon had got into his mouth and couldn't be got out, unable to walk alone in any act of his life, and patronising the sister whom he selfishly loved . . . because he suffered her to lead him.[55]

Mr Dorrit's speech is never very quick nor exact, particularly when the subject of a small 'testimonial' is concerned. He speaks to Merdle of '"the arrangement—hum—the laying out, that is to say, in the best way, of—ha, hum—my money."' The narrator comments: 'Mr. Dorrit's speech had had more hesitation in it than usual, as he approached this ticklish topic . . .'.[56] Merdle himself, of course, hardly ever has anything to say for himself. Because he has become the agent of money, even his tongue seems to have lost the power of movement: 'Mr. Merdle turned his tongue in his closed mouth—it seemed a stiff and unmanageable tongue . . .'.[57] Having paralysed his tongue and made normal self-revelation impossible, Mr Merdle has left to him only one form of signal to the world. When his economic schemes self-destruct, he is driven to open his veins in a bath-house. In contrast, John Chivery, motivated by love and not money, finds that his inability to command words is overcome by the urgency with which he scours 'a very prairie of wild words':

> 'It's all very well to trample on it, but it's there. It may be that it couldn't be trampled upon if it wasn't there. But that doesn't make it gentlemanly, that doesn't make it honourable, that doesn't justify throwing a person back upon himself after he has struggled and strived out of himself like a butterfly. The world may sneer at a turnkey, but he's a man—when he isn't a woman, which among female criminals he's expected to be.'

Ridiculous as the incoherence of his talk was, there was yet a truth-
fulness in Young John's simple, sentimental character . . .[58]

Flora Casby is a little like John Chivery; at least Dickens allows her to be
thought to have some genuine centre of feeling, which partly compensates
for her disruption of normal discourse. Flora's misuse of language is not
closely related to the money theme of the rest of the novel; she misuses
language not because she is corrupted by money (although she cannot
entirely have escaped being tainted by her father's activities), but because
she has a confused sense of time. Flora, like Mrs Clennam, has tried to stop
the clock and this suggests that they are suffering from the 'mental unheal-
thiness of almost all recluses' who are 'unable to measure the changes
beyond our view by any larger standard than the shrunken one of our own
uniform and contracted existence . . .'.[59] Flora has made 'a moral mermaid
of herself', swimming half in the past when she and Clennam were lovers,
and half in the present as the 'relict of the later Mr F.' Perhaps a less than
merciful caricature of Maria Beadnell, Flora does at least merit some tender
sympathy from Dickens.

Not so her father. Mr Casby has presented himself to the world under the
disguise of Pancks. Pancks does all the evil work in Bleeding Heart Yard.
Casby is, in short, a misleading communication; he is 'a mere Inn signpost
without any Inn—an invitation to rest and be thankful, when there was no
place to put up at, and nothing whatever to be thankful for.'[60] Pancks has
been Casby's agent, in the pejorative sense, but by the end of the novel he
has become much less mechanical, and much more active in the primary
sense. For these reasons Pancks asks if the dwellers in Bleeding Heart Yard
are acquainted with English Grammar. He then gives them the lesson as
taught by Casby:

'I wish merely to remark that the task this Proprietor has set me, has been
never to leave off conjugating the Imperative Mood Present Tense of the
verb To keep always at it. Keep thou always at. Let him keep always at
it . . .'[61]

He announces that the 'mighty fine sign-post' of 'The Casby's Head' is in
reality called 'the Sham's Arms', and Pancks trims Casby's hair to make him
more accurately fit his sign.

The Casby's Head has been a fixed sign in the language of society and the
character Casby suggests that Dickens is interested in the possibility that an
individual can become a sign; when he does he is in danger of ceasing either
to mean or to signify. It is the energy of the renewed Pancks that allows new
meaning to be read into the justifiably superannuated sign. One can take a
clue from the Casby–Pancks events, and see what is Dickens' attitude to
the question of having a fixed place in society. It is still a commonplace of
discussion of the novel, particularly of the English (as opposed to Ameri-

can) novel, and especially of the Victorian novel, that it urges on us the necessity of having a fixed part in society. Now, this is true in a very specially qualified sense: the sense in which Dorrit actively works for the benefit of her fellow human beings. Dickens is careful to differentiate this commitment from having a fixed place, however. To have a fixed place is to have given up one's agency; ultimately, as in Merdle's case, it is to commit suicide.

Fanny Dorrit has occasionally been given rhetorically to wishing herself dead, from boredom and lack of opportunity, or from embarrassment. Little Dorrit urges Fanny to lose herself in love of her intended husband: '"If you loved any one, all this feeling would change. If you loved any one, you would no more be yourself, but you would quite lose and forget yourself in your devotion to him."'[62] Fanny, however, answers: '"I know that I wish to have a more *defined and distinct* position, in which I can assert myself with greater effect against that isolent woman [Mrs Merdle]."'[63] Little Dorrit suggests a kind of permanent disguise that the loving heart always wears, and it is similar to the one adopted by John Harmon—that is, a kind of death—but Fanny has not eyes to see that kind of drama. She seeks a more fixed significance, more *definition* in the parrot language of society. She dresses up for a part in a completely different, less vital kind of play:

Now, and not before, Miss Fanny burst upon the scene completely arrayed for her new part. Now and not before she wholly absorbed Mr. Sparkler in her light, and shone for both, and twenty more. No longer feeling that want of a defined place and character which had caused her so much trouble . . .[64]

Having realised her ambition of being fixed and defined we hear the ironically questioning voice of the narrator comment: '"Happy? Fanny must have been happy. No more wishing one's self dead now."'[65] Having rejected the disguise offered by Dorrit, and the type of death she stands for, Fanny is soon seen living through the consequences of her choice of 'life'. Finding herself '"in a situation which to a certain extent disqualifies me for going into society"'—that is, finding herself pregnant—Fanny declares 'with bitterness that it really was too bad, and that positively it was enough to make one wish one was dead!'[66] Ironically, in order to attain her position of defined public eminence, in order to appear, Fanny has to keep a secret, and in this novel more than in *Dombey and Son*, secrets mean death. In their last conversation before Fanny firmly decides to marry Sparkler, Fanny cries on Little Dorrit's shoulder: 'It was the last time Fanny ever showed that there was any hidden, suppressed, or conquered feeling in her on the matter.'[67] The kind of public life Fanny seeks—a defined one—requires first a split between inner and outer, and ultimately the death of the heart, or hollowness. So, to keep a secret of this sort, is to begin to die, but not in the benign sense preached by Little Dorrit.

Chapter 10 of Part II begins with a long consideration of secrecy, too long to quote in full, in which secrecy is gradually associated with the grave. The conclusion of the passage focuses on Clennam's mother, 'firmly holding all the secrets of her own and his father's life, and austerely opposing herself, front to front, to the great final secret of all life'. Clennam, finally roused into 'a more decided course of action', takes steps to get Affery to declare her dreams: 'If she could be brought to become communicative, and to do what lay in her to break the spell of secrecy the enshrouded the house, he might shake off the paralysis of which every hour that passed over his head made him more acutely sensible.'[68] Mrs Clennam's suppression of information is magnified in her character by her general paralysis. Having chosen secrecy she has lost all real agency—although, interestingly enough, she is a business *agent*, in the secondary sense. The low fire she keeps burning in her grate suggests the suicidal nature of her suppression. The fire occasionally 'flashed up passionately, as she did; but for the most part it was suppressed, like her, and preyed upon itself evenly and slowly'.[69] Under the coercion of Rigaud-Blandois, Mrs Clennam finally explodes:

> With the set expression of her face all torn away by the explosion of her passion, and with a bursting, from every rent feature, of the smouldering fire so long pent up, she cried out: 'I will tell it myself!'[70]

This is a suppressed fire similar to the one in Louisa Gradgrind, and perhaps much more like the one in Bradley Headstone. The fire of human emotion ought to keep burning clearly outwards, because if it is denied it becomes dangerous.

The image is surely enough to convince anyone under the impression that Dickens believes in passivity and denial of vital forceful emotions to change his mind. Mrs Clennam has for too long reversed the natural flow from inner to outer to be able long to regain a proper order. Indeed she has 'reversed the order of Creation, and breathed her own breath into a clay image of her Creator'.[71] Briefly the divine order is restored as once again Mrs Clennam returns to the world of speech. As she utters words, she regains the ability to move her body:

> Many years had come and gone since she had had the free use even of her fingers; but it was noticeable that she had already more than once struck her clenched hand vigorously upon the table, and that when she said these words she raised her whole arm in the air, as though it had been a common action with her.[72]

It appears, briefly, 'almost as if a dead woman had risen'; she is a female Lazarus come back from the dead 'to tell you all'. For Dickens, the power of the word is the power of life. Mrs Clennam has had a fixed position in society, but she has not been satisfied with a too delimited one. She has so far expanded her external identity as to believe that she is God. Flintwinch is closer to the truth when he calls her 'a female Lucifer in appetite for power!'[73] Having denied the inner world, and having had nothing to say, Mrs Clennam is hollow at the core and Flintwinch notes another characteristic propensity to cannibalism: '"you want to swallow up everybody alive"'.[74] There are other brief references to the topic of cannibalism, notably the suspicion of customers that Mr F's Aunt 'had sold herself to the pie-shop to be made up, and was then sitting in the pie-shop parlour, declining to complete her contract'.[75] Mrs Clennam, the would-be devouring fiend, has, as we noted, been consuming herself by burning inwardly for too long. Once again the benign logic of Dickens' view of evil sees her disappear like others of her type. There is a divine retribution visited upon her and 'the rigid silence she had so long held was evermore enforced upon her . . .'.[76]

Miss Wade is somewhat similar to Mrs Clennam, in that she is a self-tormenting worker of minor evils, as Mrs Clennam is a self-consuming worker of major ones. Mrs Clennan fails to express heart in visible signs. She makes secrets. Miss Wade, by contrast, recognises but does not trust visible and public signs. Her egotism has insight, and she is always going beyond the obvious to discover some hidden meaning—a meaning wounding to Miss Wade's self-esteem. She looks for secrets where there are none. As she claims, '"From a very early age I have detected what those about me thought they hid from me."' She is given the power of 'habitually discerning the truth'. She makes one attempt, in the letter to Clennam, to express the very private meaning of her life for which words and common human understanding are barely adequate. She believes that a school friend who showed special kindness had a plan to make everyone fond of her and so drive Miss Wade wild with jealousy. At a school for young women, she discovers again '"Fair words and fair pretences; but I penetrated below those assertions of themselves and depreciations of me . . ."'.[77] She becomes a governess, and her kind mistress sympathises with her, feeling that Miss Wade has not been 'easy' with them, meaning 'at ease'. Miss Wade takes up the other meaning, not on an equal social footing: '"Oh! You are such great people, my lady," said I.' Her mistress replies '"I am unfortunate in using a word which may convey a meaning—and evidently does—quite opposite to my intention."'[78]

Miss Wade, in short, is an example of the painful results of misreading. She believes herself possessed of powerful insight—of an extraordinary ability to read between the lines. In the discussion of *Dombey and Son*, we saw that Dickens can argue that it is necessary to go beyond signs in order to seize the imaginative content, the speaker's meaning rather than the word's meaning. This attitude was seen to entail an occasional comical contempt for mere signs (or signifiers). Miss Wade provides the necessary qualification to that view. If one distrusts the visible and public in favour of a too particular personal interpretation, one will miss the intention altogether.

Miss Wade suffers, as the page heading tells us, from 'Distorted Vision'. She had at one time a young lover, and she fantasises a relationship between them that Dickens seems to intend to be reminiscent of that between Dombey and Edith. His admiration for her worried her:

'He took no pains to hide it; and caused me to feel among the rich people as if he had bought me for my looks, and made a show of his purchase to justify himself. They appraised me in their own minds, I saw, and were curious to ascertain what my full value was. I resolved that they should not know. I was immovable and silent before them; and would have suffered any one of them to kill me sooner than I would have laid myself out to bespeak their approval.'[79]

The role of Miss Wade in the story is to reassert Dickens' belief in the necessity of some form of public revelation of self, so that one does not have to fall back on the impossible attempt to know by oneself what is in other minds—a gulf impassable without trust in words. Properly used and trusted, language, or the artful use of language to express the heart, provides a public ritual with none of the risks of the fixed and defined position in society sought by Fanny.

Having worked laboriously through all possible attitudes to fiction in *Dombey and Son*, Dickens is much more at ease with the theme in *Little Dorrit*. Mrs Clennam and Miss Wade both make unacceptable fictions. Arthur Clennam has suffered from the absence of fictions of positive value in his youth, and this has led to his relative ineffectuality in life:

At no Mother's knee but hers had he ever dwelt in his youth on hopeful promises, on playful fancies, on the harvests of tenderness and humility that lie hidden in the early-fostered seeds of the imagination; on the oaks of retreat from blighting winds, that have the germs of their strong roots in nursery acorns.[80]

Under Little Dorrit's influence—and she is given to express herself in story, as is witnessed by the story of the Princess she tells to Maggie—he will mend. Indeed, because he does not have a developed and balanced sense of romance, he is unwise enough to take on the Circumlocution Office. As the young Barnacle warns him: '"our place is not a wicked Giant to be charged at full tilt; but only a windmill showing you, as it grinds immense quantities of chaff, which way the country wind blows."'[81] With his Signor Panco, or Sancho Panza, Quixote-Clennam has a try, only to fail.

The wiser artisan, Doyce, more skilled in the ways of the world, as well as more imaginative, has warned him off and Dickens seems to insist that fancy is not a merely Quixotic thing; it is immensely practical. Those who believe, like Meagles, that Doyce must be a duffer are very wide of the mark. Amidst all the difficulties of secrecy, ambiguity, misread intentions and the possible distortions of fiction (or of 'castle-building', as the egotistic version of 'making' is so often called) Doyce can do the one thing needful. He spells out exactly what is Dickens' obsessive concern in his novels:

> He had the power, often to be found in union with such a character, of explaining what he himself perceived, and meant, with the direct force and distinctness with which it struck his own mind. His manner of demonstration was so orderly and neat and simple, that it was not easy to mistake him. There was something almost ludicrous in the complete irreconcilability of a vague conventional notion that he must be a visionary man, with the precise, sagacious travelling of his eye and thumb over the plans, their patient stoppages at particular points, their careful returns to other points whence little channels of explanation had to be traced up, and his steady manner of making everything good and everything sound at each important stage, before taking his bearer on a line's-breadth further. His dismissal of himself from his description, was hardly less remarkable. He never said, I discovered this adaptation or invented that combination; but showed the whole thing as if the Divine artificer had made it, and he had happened to find it . . .[82]

The description is a useful guide to Dickens' own method. The many little channels of explanation are carefully followed up and seen to join the main stream. And it can be seen that many of Dickens' sub-plots are there for the purpose of explaining, or investigating further, a central idea. While certainly not as detached as Joyce's artist, paring his nails on a cloud, there is a sense that Dickens' art does refine the artist's personality out of existence: at the very least it is dramatically mediated to us by many characters. The vague conventional notion of Dickens as a sentimental, enthusiastic visionary with no practical solution for society's evils need not perhaps be totally given up by those fond of such a Dickens—but such a view certainly needs to be modified by recognising the Doyce in Dickens: the practical man who can see that the solutions of society's problems, as well as many of the problems themselves, lie first of all in one's relation to language.

Miss Wade's difficulties with reading between the lines proves an easy point of transition to some of the central themes of *Our Mutual Friend*. The novel is too complex and rich to be fully treated here, but the themes we have been following in Dickens' work can be seen to reappear here, and they do turn out to be of central importance to the novel. The problems of reading are closely allied to the problem of agency, and the problems of being an agent, or actor, are treated openly in terms of the theatre: as if one had to be a theatrical actor in order to be an agent. Wrayburn himself, in a curious parenthetical comment to his friend Mortimer Lightwood, provides a gloss on the importance of Reading:

'You charm me, Mortimer, with your reading of my weaknesses. (By-the-way, that very word, Reading, in its critical use, always charms me. An actress's Reading of a chambermaid, a dancer's Reading of a hornpipe, a singer's Reading of a song, a marine painter's Reading of the sea, the kettle-drum's Reading of an instrumental passage, are phrases ever youthful and delightful.'[83]

Since Wrayburn himself never again takes up the topic, it is perhaps safe to assume that we have here Dickens himself briefly speaking of his own interests through Wrayburn. The world itself is obviously constituted by the act of reading, and reading is never a passive affair. An actress's 'reading' is clearly an enactment in her own person; it is an interpretation acted out.

Wrayburn himself is a very poor reader, particularly of his own motives. Unable to follow Lightwood's advice to 'look on to the end' it seems as if Wrayburn 'actually did not know what to make of himself'.[84] He fits out a domestic-looking flat and invites Mortimer to view it. Quizzed by him, Wrayburn denies that he intends either to capture and desert Lizzy Hexam, or to marry her, or to pursue her. As he says, '"My dear fellow, I don't design anything. I have no design whatever. I am incapable of designs. If I conceived a design, I should speedily abandon it, exhausted by the operation."'[85] This might seem to be mere talk on Wrayburn's part, but it is true; he cannot read himself well enough to know what he intends towards Lizzy. Lizzy herself is clear enough, however. She runs away and when Wrayburn finally tracks her down she says to him '"to tell me why you came here, is to put me to shame!"'[86] Wrayburn's unacknowledged intention—unacknowledged because he is unaware of it—has been to make Lizzy his mistress. As Lightwood repeatedly informs us, Wrayburn is absurd and he is 'not a consistent fellow'.[87] The reason he is inconsistent, and potentially harmful to Lizzy, is that he is a poor reader of his own motives and that he is a passive character. Or to put it in the terms that will later be seen to be used for John Harmon, Wrayburn passively plays an active part in the world. Harmon, by contrast, forces himself 'to act a passive part'.[88]

When we first see Wrayburn he is as if dead, 'buried alive in the back of his chair'.[89] Buried by his life in the society of Veneerings, it is no wonder that he cannot get his signals straight, for as the Inspector says about a corpse, 'you never got a sign out of bodies'.[90] This state of death-in-life results from Wrayburn's acceptance of a position in life that has been forced on him by others. His father, according to his system of arranging his children's lives, '"pre-arranged for myself that I was to be the barrister I am . . . and also the married man I am not"'. Once having accepted this external 'definition', despite the fact that he hates his profession, Wrayburn continues to live on the perquisites of his superior social rank and to eschew precisely what might bring him into a fully active life: '"If there is a word in the dictionary under any letter from A to Z that I abominate, it is energy."'[91]

Occasionally this sense of rank will lead him into a type of acting, but he performs on a corrupt stage. When Lizzy is being aided by Riah, Wrayburn deliberately insults him in tone and manner, choosing to neglect his real name and call him 'Aaron' instead. He is exercising his power over Lizzy and displaying his prowess to the world as it presents itself in the person of 'Aaron': 'But now, that his part was played out for the evening, and when in turning his back upon the Jew he came off the stage, he was thoughtful.'[92] On occasions like this, Wrayburn is clearly a melodramatic villain belonging in the company of Wegg—who is a 'professional' reader, and 'declines and falls' for Boffin—who has a 'stage-ballet manner'; or in the company of the Lammles who stage a drama between Fledgeby and Georgina Podsnap, and then proceed to act all the parts by putting words into the mouths of their puppets. Lammle is referred to as Mephistopheles[93] and we see him at one point in the characteristic action of hollow men, devouring his fellows, or at least wishing to. Mrs Lammle sees 'her dark lord engaged in an act of violence with a bottle of soda-water as though he were wringing the neck of some unlucky creature and pouring its blood down his throat'.[94]

Wrayburn's playing of a false part arises directly from his inconsistency and passivity. Indeed inconsistency is seen to be itself a form of passivity, since there is no conscious acting upon known motives. The pun that Dickens uses in this novel is that passion is also a form of passivity. The love that Wrayburn has for Lizzy is potentially corrupting because it is not active and self-transcending; it is a passion and passions take control of one's voluntary self. His passion for Lizzy works against the set of his personality as a careless involuntary barrister of superior social standing. The two passivities divide him. Just before he is attacked by Headstone, Wrayburn expresses his dilemma: '"Out of the question to marry her . . . and out of the question to leave her. The crisis!"'[95] Immediately upon so expressing his 'crisis', he is attacked by Headstone, and then a short time later pulled out of the water by Lizzy. The many instances of 'death by water' in the novel are meant to express once again the need to be baptised into life by a kind of death. Facing mortality can jolt the careless and the involuntary into a new awareness of the need for energy in life, and in Wrayburn's case the 'death' he suffers is the death of his social self. It is murdered out of him and when he awakes he is purified into singleness, which he expresses by means of the one word 'Wife'. One needs to exercise careful discrimination at this point, in order to see that when Dickens dismisses passion as potentially evil, and has his characters choose marriage, he is not merely catering to Victorian prudery or middle-class morality—although he can usually manage to do that as well. Marriage is for Dickens anything but a social relationship, in the negative sense of the word. It is a willed union of two consciously loving beings, best expressed in this novel by Bella and John. The fact that marriages are so often prodigiously reproductive is not necessarily an indication of Dickens' comfortable domesticity either. Rather it indicates that once there has been a marriage of true minds and hearts and once the involuntarism of passion has been overcome, a rich sexuality is released in a newly created kind of drama.

Headstone's 'killing' of Wrayburn leads very quickly to his own death, as Rogue Riderhood, believing himself immune to drowning, and he pull each other under the waters of the lock. In a sense, in attacking Wrayburn, Headstone kills himself. The close identification of Headstone and Wrayburn is established in the hunter–hunted part of the novel, in which their psychological entanglement makes them for a time virtually indistinguishable. Indeed, the only difference between them is that Headstone is striving for the social rank that Wrayburn already has. Headstone forces on himself the passivity of a fixed role in society that Wrayburn has allowed others to force onto him. Bradley lives in a kind of false theatre, or circus, which imprisons him: 'Tied up all day with his disciplined show upon him, subdued to the performance of his routine of educational tricks, encircled by a gabbling crowd, he broke loose at night like an ill-tamed wild animal.'[96] Bradley is trying to force himself into immobility, but as yet he has not been able fully to kill off the human emotions, which, as Dickens demonstrates again, have an enormous and undeniable energy. He has not yet fully been able to emasculate himself, but he is trying.

As part of his plan to define himself, Bradley adopts an unchanging mode of dress: 'He was never seen in any other dress, and yet there was a certain stiffness in his manner of wearing this, as there were a want of adaptation between him and it, recalling some mechanics in their holiday clothes.'[97] (Compare the description of Lady Tippins' clothes on p. 164.) This lack of fit is on the way to being corrected, it would seem, as Bradley's body itself—moving beyond his conscious active control—begins to hollow itself out. At Riderhood's lock he throws himself into a chair and 'a great spirt of blood burst from his nose'. This has happened '"twice—three times—four times—I don't know how many times—since last night"'.[98] The passion leading him to murder Wrayburn is obviously draining him of his own vital humanity, and it may be that it is only a suit of clothes that is drowned in that final plunge.

Headstone makes clear Dickens' intention to identify passion with the absence of agency and to demonstrate that the fact of being powerfully moved, and the resultant ability to do a lot of evil in the world, is not equivalent to achieving the state of agency in the primary sense. In the first exchange between Headstone and Wrayburn, Wrayburn comments that Headstone appears 'to be rather too passionate for a good schoolmaster'. Headstone picks up the word and it is the central topic of the whole passage:

'Oh, what a misfortune is mine,' cried Bradley, breaking off to wipe the starting perspiration from his face as he shook from head to foot, 'that I cannot so control myself as to appear a stronger creature than this, when a man who has not felt in all his life what I have felt in a day can so command himself!' He said it in a very agony, and even followed it with an errant motion of his hands as if he could have torn himself.[99]

Passion is equivalent to being out of control of oneself, and to that extent it denies agency. The passage indicates also, however, why one has perhaps more sympathy for Headstone than for Wrayburn. Wrayburn is able to exercise greater self-control only because he is a lesser man as far as emotional life is concerned. Dickens might well be echoing Blake's sentiment and suggesting that Wrayburn's prudence, or self-control, is really an ugly old maid courted by incapacity. To surrender one's agency, however, is clearly suicidal, as can be seen by Headstone's tendency to tear himself. As he attempts to propose to Lizzy, he tells her that '"it is not voluntary in me to be here now"'.[100] He feels a 'resentful shame to find himself defeated by this passion' for Lizzy. He has discovered that 'the power of self-command had departed from him'.[101]

Repressed for so long, his natural instincts have built up a terrific and terrible power of their own. Dickens' point is not, it is worth repeating, that strong feelings, even strong sexual feelings, are bad. On the contrary, it is the denial of these feelings that produces evil results of the sort we see in Headstone. In part it is Headstone's inability to understand a particular word in the dictionary—as it is Wrayburn's (energy, in his case)—that signals his trouble. He says to Lizzy:

'You know what I am going to say. I love you. What other men may mean when they use that expression, I cannot tell; what *I* mean is, that I am under the influence of some tremendous attraction which I have resisted in vain, and which overmasters me.'[102]

He explains his difficulties with language further: '"It is another of my miseries that I cannot speak to you or speak of you without stumbling at every syllable, unless I let the check go altogether and run mad."'[103] When he loses all self-government, the 'wild energy of the man, now quite let loose, was absolutely terrible'.[104] Headstone's passion is inarticulate and terrible—and it is terrible in part because it is inarticulate. Passion needs natural and continuing expression—and it needs mediation. It requires the mediation of the one word Headstone cannot understand: love.

There are one or two other obvious examples of distortion of personality in the novel; the distortion signalled again by misuse of language. Veneering, who remains only on the social surface of life, and as a result has really nothing to say from his inner depths, makes a speech to the electors of the borough of Pocket-Breeches that is described as 'a neat and appropriate stammer'. He quickly 'loses his way in the usual No Thoroughfares of speech' and 'institutes an original comparison between the country, and a ship; pointedly calling the ship, the Vessel of the State, and the Minister the Man at the Helm'.[105] Interestingly enough, Dickens' irony at Veneering's expense backfires a little, for he holds up for scorn the very cliché that he himself makes so much use of in his later novels, especially in *Little Dorrit* with its Barnacles clinging to the ship of State. It may be that Dickens' own analysis of politics and society is being recognised as itself perhaps somewhat trite, or clichéd, or perhaps of secondary importance to the psychological investigations he can pursue by means of images of oceans, rivers, depths and surfaces. To put a vessel of State on an ocean is to turn into political allegory what could have a much richer psychological significance.

Mrs Wilfer is another linguistic offender. Having used the word 'attractions' in speaking of her daughter Bella and having seen John Harmon neatly pick up the word and add to the implicit compliment, Mrs Wilfer backpedals furiously:

> 'Pardon me,' returned Mrs. Wilfer, with dreadful solemnity, 'but I had not finished.'
> 'Pray excuse me.'
> 'I was about to say,' pursued Mrs. Wilfer, who clearly had not had the faintest idea of saying anything more: 'that when I use the term attractions, I do so with the qualification that I do not mean it in any way whatever.'[106]

If Carker suggested the Cheshire cat to Lewis Carroll, then one might also suggest that Dickens is the source of Humpty-Dumpty's claim that when he uses a word it means whatever he chooses it to mean. Mrs Wilfer goes one better than Humpty: she means nothing at all when she uses a word.

Less selfish people have less difficulty with language. Boffin confidently sets out to discover the world hidden in the written word, and finds quickly that there is a great number of 'Scarers in Print'. Surprised perhaps, but undaunted he declares, '"But I'm in for it now!"'[107] When he is in the midst of the stories about misers, he encounters another difficulty: 'What to believe, in the course of his reading, was Mr. Boffin's chief literary difficulty indeed. . .'.[108] The whole episode of Boffin's apprenticeship to the misers is a tricky one for Dickens' readers, who, for the most part, do not know what to believe. In the postscript Dickens explains that he took no pains to delude his readers about John Harmon, but he certainly does take pains to have them believe, with Bella, that Boffin has changed his nature under the influence of this wealth. As it turns out, of course, we have been misreading—at least we must conclude that this is Dickens' point. This aspect of the novel is perhaps least satisfying, and a reader with less good nature than Bella is bound to feel that some important information has been held back from him. A novelist who takes as his theme the evils of secrecy is bound to find consistency difficult to come by, because up to a point the success of the narrative requires that he keeps certain things secret until the appropriate time of expression arrives. Occasionally he must succumb to a miserly temptation.

Boffin's fiction, however, fits neatly into the group of justified and benign fictions that are intended to work good for others—and one is perhaps never more aware of the patronising tone always latent in Dickens' analysis of fictional truths. The little act that he puts on grows directly out of his own and Mrs Boffin's innocent delight in the world. They both characteristically behave as if 'the principal streets were a great Theatre and the play were childishly new to them. . .'.[109] So much under the influence of John Harmon's self-effacing goodness, we can assume that the Boffin's submergence of themselves in their adopted roles belongs with John's decision to 'act a passive part'. In this kind of freely-improvised theatre, or fiction, selfishness is overcome because, it seems, the self is presented only indirectly; it is mediated by means of a demonstration that will present truth for apprehension, but will not enforce it upon the unwilling. Bella proves her worth by apprehending the truth of the fiction, even though she cannot at first see through the fictional drama.

Riah is freed from Fledgeby as the result of a theatrically presented truth as well. As ideal a Jew as he is intended to be, one is a little uneasy—as is Jenny Wren—with Riah's passive endurance of Fledgeby's malign fiction. If it is unacceptable for one passively to wear the mask, or role, assigned to one by society, then it must be equally inappropriate to allow oneself to be used as a mask and as far as Fledgeby is concerned, 'Mr. Riah is his mask'.[110] Mr Riah fulfils his task by being a reader, perhaps a better reader than he ought to be in the circumstances. Fledgeby never signals anything to Riah, except indirectly and by means of silences. Riah must interpret these indirect signallings and act upon them. On one occasion he comes to a decision to act after he has closely 'read his master's face and learnt the book'.[111] Ultimately, Riah breaks out of this too passive role which requires him to be too active an agent in the secondary sense. He explains his particularly painful situation to Jenny and shows why people were ready to believe evil of him:

'And passing the painful scene of that day in review before me many times, I always saw that the poor gentleman believed the story readily, because I was one of the Jews—that you believed the story readily, my child, because I was one of the Jews—that the story itself first came into the invention of the originator thereof, because I was one of the Jews. This was the result of my having had you three before me, face to face, and seeing the thing visibly presented as upon a theatre. Wherefore I perceived that the obligation was upon me to leave this service.'[112]

Theatre here is like the acceptable use of language for fiction: both are, at their best, the creative construction and presentation of a truth which is

accessible by no other means. Fiction has a much higher task than the
passive one of reflecting Victorian society.

John Harmon has already been discussed in passing, and one should
notice briefly the way in which he embodies the major pattern of meaning
for the novel. He dies and is reborn in a new identity, and persists in
artificial mediation of himself throughout the story, until forced into revelation at the last minute, partly in order to provide the happy ending
Dickens requires. Harmon is thrown into the river and nearly killed. He
returns from this baptismal plunge to live a life permanently mediated by an
identity that is an artistic creation. He plays a drama in order to keep his
own selfish tendencies under control. He has adopted a second self as a
self-imposed theatrical discipline. Unlike Bradley Headstone, in this reborn
state he never lacks self-government. Bradley has never submerged himself
in his inner depths and is shocked to discover he has any. Under the
influence of Lizzy '"the bottom of this raging sea"', striking himself upon
the breast, "has been heaved up ever since"'.[113] When Bradley takes his
final plunge with Riderhood, it is to be expected that he will never surface.
Harmon has had his merely social identity—as inheritor of a fortune and a
position—murdered conveniently out of him. He plunges into his own
inner resources and—this is most important—resurfaces. Miss Wade, we
saw, was able to go into depths even where there were none, but she never
was able fully to rise to the surface of public life again. The journey into the
interior is essential, but the travellers into those inner jungles must come
out. Naked savages must put on some kind of clothing. Intentions must be
manifested in language.

By acting a passive part—rather than passively playing an active
part—Harmon creates a situation in which significant contact with others is
possible. Fortunately for him, Bella proves that she has the inner resources
required. She discovers them fully only when she chooses to murder that
potential self she is as a recipient of wealth and position from Boffin. Once
they have both reached the stage of being able to participate in the free
drama of life, we discover that sexuality—as opposed to mere passion—is
freed and Bella is quickly pregnant. In her new home, for which she
develops a 'genius', she would put 'back her hair with both hands, as if she
were making the most business-like arrangements for going dramatically
distracted, would enter on the household affairs of the day'.[114] This new
domestic drama (J. Hillis Miller discusses this domestic drama in *The Form of
Victorian Fiction*) is the end result of the new discipline of expression
discovered by John Harmon. It is important to recall that the drug he was
given by his assailants had a peculiar, lingering effect. He says, '"I had no
notion where I was, and could not articulate—through the poison that had
made me insensible having affected my speech . . ."'. The effect gradually,
but never completely disappears:

'That suffering has gradually weakened and weakened since, and has only come upon me by starts, and I hope I am free from it now; but even now, I have sometimes to think, constrain myself, and stop before speaking, or I could not say the words I want to say.'[115]

Here is no prairie of wild words, nor is there the opposite condition of Headstone who can barely at all 'grind out' the words necessary to make himself intelligible. Rather we see a state which suggests what is necessary for all, the careful and conscious direction of one's expressions in order to overcome any potential difficulties that may be caused by either the vehicle of expression, or the person who is being expressed. Harmon also suggests the effort that goes into the achievement of a state of creative expression. For angelic figures such as Lizzy Hexam many of the difficulties seem to disappear as a result of purity of heart and intention. Nevertheless the act of appearing is a courageous one: 'Bella sat enchained by the deep, unselfish passion of this girl or woman of her own age, courageously revealing itself in the confidence of her sympathetic perception of its truth.'[116] Under the influence of a nature that courageously reveals itself, Wrayburn too struggles to the surface to be reborn:

> This frequent rising of a drowning man from the deep, was dreadful to the beholders . . . His desire to impart something that was on his mind, his unspeakable yearning to have speech with his friend and make a communication to him, so troubled him when he recovered consciousness, that its term was thereby shortened.[117]

Soon, however, Wrayburn surfaces long enough to appear once again in language, using the one other word he has been able to utter significantly: 'Wife'.

It is possible to see how Dickens' conscious and persistent pursuit of the ideas inherent in the word 'agent' leads to the complexity and importance of his later novels. He begins, perhaps, with a simple faith, which he never loses, in the essential value of energy and the act. He is led to pun on the two senses of agency and then to investigate the very troubling fact that all acts, particularly acts of fiction, depend on mediation by language. This leads to a consideration of the arbitrariness and ambiguity of signs and to the problems of reading and interpretation. The whole world is seen, as Carlyle sees it in *Sartor Resartus*, as a clothing of signs which, properly read, will reveal an inner truth. Dickens approaches the problem in a significantly different way from Carlyle. He focuses again and again on the way in which hollow clothes can suggest an inner meaning that does not exist; or on the way in which an over-active perception will read meanings not justified by the surface signs. The difficulties of reading are difficulties of surface and depth. For those like Veneering who remain on the surface of social life, living will always be a matter of death-in-life. They must take the plunge. As Jung suggests, full development of the self can only take place when the individual descends into the underworld of the shadow and discovers the secrets of the personality hidden from the conscious mind. The descent into the underworld requires a golden bough of some sort, however, to guarantee return to the surface. Dickens' analysis of fictional language finally reaches a consistent and powerfully significant synthesis in his last books with his discovery of the way in which to articulate surface and depth in the theatre of the world.

6 George Eliot: The Invisible Fabrick and the Clothes of Time

George Eliot provides points of contact with almost all the authors and themes we have considered so far, which is one measure of her significance in the history of the novel. Perhaps she is closest to Jane Austen, one author who aroused her animosity, but who influenced her a great deal nevertheless. Both are centrally concerned with the way in which the active imagination must be clearly aware of the external ground on which it is going to act, if the acts are to be significant. Eliot's two most important themes are an analysis of the nature of action (and therefore also of passion) and the complicating fact that men live by interpreting signs that are ambiguous and cannot contain all that they wish to say. Like Dickens, she learns to trust art to overcome distances and her later novels, particularly *Daniel Deronda*, show evidence of an increasing visionary quality, a belief that there is something behind the visible that we can contact. What begins in her early career as a feeling that we must discern the meaning behind the signs (written and spoken) is transmuted by her interest in Time: Deronda, under Mordecai's tutelage, seems on the verge of responding to a message which has not yet been written. That book closes (wisely perhaps) as Deronda is about to begin to act so as to bring a new vision into material reality. In one of her favourite authors (at least so far as one can judge from the number of times she quotes from him in her novels), Sir Thomas Browne, we find the following:

> The severe Schools shall never laugh me out of the Philosophy of Hermes, that this visible World is but a Picture of the invisible, wherein, as in a Pourtraict, things are not truely, but in equivocal shapes, and as they counterfeit some more real substance in that invisible fabrick.[1]

This is, of course, a version of Paul's claim that here below we see but as through a glass darkly. Eliot's hermetic beliefs do not amount to a claim that we can see God beneath His works; for her, humanism replaces God, and what the interpreter can see behind the signs is human being, intention and motive. If the signs are the product of a full and loving imagination, then they become active and aid one in seeing beyond to that other hidden 'fabrick'. Not surprisingly, we find Eliot quoting the same passage from Milton with which we began (p.1). Deronda is about to come into possession of papers left by his father which will open his past life to him

> The moment wrought strongly on Deronda's imaginative susceptibility: in the presence of one linked still in zealous friendship with the grandfather whose hope had yearned towards him when he was unborn, and who though dead was yet to speak with him in those written memorials which, says Milton, 'contain a potency of life in them to be as active as that soul whose progeny they are', he seemed to himself to be touching the electric chain of his own ancestry . . .[2]

The achievement of such active progeny is, however, the end result of a long spiritual process, which for Eliot is at least as much a psychological as a spiritual journey. Her earlier works are explorations into the implications of her belief that the complete human individual is fulfilled only by means of action and her recognition that such action is often frustrated by the very circumstances which seem to demand it. When Hetty Sorel has firmly bound herself in the mesh of the law, Adam Bede finds that there is no outlet for his need for action:

> This brave active man, who would have hastened towards any danger or toil to rescue Hetty from an apprehended wrong or misfortune, felt himself powerless to contemplate irremediable evil and suffering. The susceptibility which would have been an impelling force where there was any possibility of action, became helpless anguish when he was obliged to be passive, or else sought an active outlet in the thought of inflicting justice on Arthur.[3]

The impasse here is an important one. It serves in part to convey Eliot's interest in the relation (or lack of relation) between motive and ground. The lack of fit between Adam's need for active expression and the possibilities in the situation for significant action arises because the situation is one in which only Hetty's action could be significant. It is not Adam's scene. Further, the scene is a necessary one to reveal further to Adam that he has been misreading Hetty's character. He discovers that surface appearances are misleading and by means of his suffering he learns to see into depths and so discover the real value of Dinah the Methodist preacher *pro temps*. The novel presents us two of Eliot's ideals: the active individual (and one must remember that Dinah also is active) and the individual with personal depth. Just as Adam must learn how to read signs, so too Dinah must emerge from her depths and learn how to recognise a sign when she sees one, and when she does she gives up her vocation as Methodist preacher to become the lover of Adam.

Both Hetty and her lover Arthur Donnithorne (the thorny gift?) act from a

surface sense of things only. Hetty, we learn, 'often took the opportunity
. . . of looking at the pleasing reflection of herself in those polished surfaces'[4] (of polished tables, pewter, made reflective by the labour of others).
Arthur is 'of an impressible nature, and lived a great deal in other people's
opinions and feelings concerning himself'.[5] He looks in the faces of others
to see his own reflection. Dinah is exactly the opposite. She seems 'as
unconscious of her outward appearance as a little boy' and has eyes which
'seemed rather to be shedding love than making observations; they had the
liquid look which tells that the mind is full of what it has to give out, rather
than impressed by external objects'.[6] When Arthur and Hetty act, they are
caught up in a ritual which in fact enforces passivity on them. As Adam
suggests, Arthur has been acting a part.[7] The false theatricality of their
contact is suggested by the likening of them to Eros and Psyche: 'he may be
Eros himself, sipping the lips of Psyche—it is all one.'[8] It is all one, the
phrase suggests the lack of individual volition in this love-making.

Eliot's critique of passion amounts to pointing out that it implies passivity, as we see at the moment when Arthur's intention is overcome:

> Ah, he doesn't know in the least what he is saying. This is not what he
> meant to say. His arm is stealing round the waist again, it is tightening its
> clasp; he is bending his face nearer and nearer . . . and for a long moment
> time has vanished.[9]

The moment may be long, but time does not vanish, and with its return
come the consequences of even such passive activity. Arthur finds himself
in a topsy-turvy world where he becomes the object of his own unwilled
act: 'His deed was reacting upon him . . .'.[10] Now, the point of all of this is
not that Eliot is warning us against sex. Her interest is a more philosophical
one. She is considering the nature of the individual personality which is
unconscious of its own motives. The fact is that a man 'carries within
him the germ of his most exceptional action' and that the acting out of
these germs has consequences, which 'are unpitying'. There is an 'unrecog-
nised agent secretly busy in Arthur's mind'.[11] Hetty too has been
unconsciously preparing consequences for herself because of her failure to
be a conscious agent. Her eventual destruction is suggested in a familiar
metaphor:

> It is too painful to think that she is a woman, with a woman's destiny
> before her—a woman spinning in young ignorance a light web of folly
> and vain hopes which may one day close round her and press upon her, *a
> rancorous poisoned garment*, changing all at once her fluttering, trivial
> butterfly sensations into a life of deep human anguish.[12]

Adam is obviously enough an overt agent with a 'habitual impatience of
mere passivity'. Nevertheless, he is open to misreading circumstances, as is

the most innocent of us. He figures to himself at one point the delight of winning 'a sweet bride like Hetty':

> Every man under such circumstances is conscious of being a great physiognomist. Nature, he knows, has a language of her own, which she uses with strict veracity, and he considers himself an adept in the language. Nature has written out his bride's character for him in those exquisite lines of cheek and lip and chin . . .[13]

In so far as he is a mere physiognomist, Adam too acts from a surface interpretation of life. The apparent, Wordsworthian, praise of Nature in the above passage is given a more characteristic, and ironic Eliot commentary a little further on:

> After all, I believe the wisest of us must be beguiled in this way sometimes, and must think both better and worse of people than they deserve. Nature has her language, and she is not unveracious; but we don't know all the intricacies of her syntax just yet, and in a hasty reading we may happen to extract the very opposite of her real meaning.[14]

Adam learns to love Dinah better as a result of learning how to read the ambiguous and misleading language of nature, and this is a consequence of his own internal deepening: 'Tender and deep as his love for Hetty had been . . . his love for Dinah was better and more precious to him; for it was the outgrowth of that fuller life which had come to him from his acquaintance with deep sorrow.'[15] Adam is an ideal character, but, though deep, he must become deeper and so a better reader.

Characteristically the theme of education, as in so many nineteenth-century novels, is a process not of learning to read the signs only, but learning also to see behind them to the depths which give them meaning. Dinah carries the fullest weight of this central topic, and it is related to her vocation: she is a speaker. She is a full mind that gives out. The power of her sermon is like 'a drama—for there is this sort of fascination in all sincere unpremeditated eloquence, which opens to one the inward drama of the speaker's emotions . . .'.[16] Despite this degree of adequacy of her eloquence, or perhaps as a result of it, Dinah is aware of the deficiencies of language for expression: ' "for we can't say half what we feel, with all our words." '[17] The narrator echoes this point about words:

> Examine your words well, and you will find that even when you have no motive to be false, it is a very hard thing to say the exact truth, even about your own immediate feelings—much harder than to say something fine about them which is *not* the exact truth.[18]

This sums up the one point of the novel, and perhaps of Eliot's vision as a whole: men must be active, but their acts are mediated. Awareness of motive, and a skilful and active attempt to embody that motive in whatever medium (which requires a conscious knowledge of the external medium as well, of course) will not necessarily succeed. Eliot, though, despite the realism with which she shows the distance between inner and outer, is also an optimist and the novel testifies to her belief that the willing heart can overcome the deficiency of signs. When Adam visits Hall Farm at one point, he and Hetty pick currants. Although neither speaks, Adam believes—he is over-reading signs again—that Hetty knows how full his heart is:

It was to Adam the time that a man can least forget in after-life,—the time when he believes that the first woman he has ever loved betrays by a slight something . . . that she is at least beginning to love him in return. The sign is so slight, it is scarcely perceptible to the ear or eye . . . it is a mere feather-touch, yet it seems to have changed his whole being . . .[19]

Adam's error will knit no rancorous garment for him, and indeed his inner fullness is the very thing that will make even the smallest of signals function miraculously. What is required is reciprocity; this he finds in Dinah. If you will think of love, says the narrator:

you will no more think the slight words, the timid looks, the tremulous touches, by which two human souls approach each other gradually, like two little quivering rainstreams, before they mingle into one—you will no more think these things trivial than you will think the first-detected signs of coming spring trivial. . . . Those slight words and looks and touches are part of the soul's language; and the finest language, I believe, is chiefly made up of unimposing words, such as 'light,' 'sound,' 'stars,' 'music,'—words really not worth looking at, or hearing, in themselves, any more than 'chips' or 'sawdust:' it is only that they happen to be the signs of something unspeakably great and beautiful.[20]

This great and beautiful thing is love, and it takes even Dinah a little time to read the apparently insignificant signals, partly because she is not used to listening to her own feelings. Adam persuades her, however: ' "if you love me so as to be willing to be nearer to me than to other people, isn't that a sign that it's right for you to change your life?" '[21]

Adam Bede, then, may be regarded as a sort of prose–Wordsworthian romance, but one does not get near its central strain until one sees that it is much more an analysis of language and the relationship of the active human spirit to the need to be embodied in signs. One can make a similar comment on *Felix Holt*. Its political analysis is only a sub-topic; the focus of the most authorial energy is once again on creating an active *persona*, or a *persona* of action, in order to express Eliot's need for expression and to further her 'philosophical' analysis of language. Felix himself and his mentor Mr Lyons are both embodiments of the power of the word. Felix, like Adam, is manly and active; he is, as Mr Lyons at first suspects, 'a roughly written page'. Mr Lyons also detects in Felix ' "a certain licence in his language, which I shall use my efforts to correct" '. The licence in his language obviously related to the fact that he runs afoul of the law, but the nature of this relationship is important to consider. Eliot's point is not that just as the would-be revolutionary must be imprisoned, so too must the too-licenced speaker learn to curb his tongue; just the opposite is the case. Felix's stint in prison is nothing more than the merest nod to the need for realism in the plot; he comes out having survived the trial of his spirit and is even more dedicated to his task than before. Eliot is concerned to show that even the power of speech has its limits. The word is powerful, but it is most powerful in realms of spirit, soul, mind, or psyche. When the inner revolution takes place that Victorian novelists are always accused of offering as a compromise for real social revolution, it is true that no significant social change may take place. Felix Holt has personal power, and he learns that there are external limits to this power, and that when he crosses the limits he may suffer. That he continues to choose to take this chance is a clear indication of Eliot's attitude to those who might counsel conservative quietude.

Mr Lyons himself does not really see any fault in Felix; he even believes that there is an advantage in being a roughly written page, as if the deficiency in the making of the surface signs provided an interesting comment on the fact that the spirit of the message comes through in any case:

> 'I abstain from judging by the outward appearance only,' he answered, with the usual simplicity. 'I myself have experienced that when the spirit is much exercised it is difficult to remember neck-bands and strings and such small accidents of our vesture, which are nevertheless decent and needful so long as we sojourn in the flesh.'[22]

If he attempts to correct Felix's excesses, it is not out of a motive of political caution, but in order to protect him from *spiritual* errors, especially of 'pride and scorn'. He himself shares Felix's delight in the power of the word:

> 'It is good that you should use plainness of speech, and I am not of those who would enforce a submissive silence on the young, that they themselves, being elders, may be heard at large; for Elihu was the youngest of Job's friend, yet was there a wise rebuke in his words; and the aged Eli was taught by a revelation to the boy Samuel. I have to keep a special watch over myself in this matter, inasmuch as I have a need of utterance which makes the thought within me seem as a pent-up fire, until I have shot it forth, as it were, in arrowy words, each one hitting its mark. Therefore I pray for a listening spirit, which is a great mark of grace.'[23]

Clearly we can detect some of the author herself in this passage. Lyons, like an artist in words, searches for a more exact rendering of the inner world:

> 'I am an eager seeker for precision, and would fain find language subtle enough to follow the utmost intricacies of the soul's pathways, but I see not why a round word that means some object, made and blessed by the Creator, should be branded and banished as a malefactor.'[24]

Society and politics ought to model themselves on language, and not the other way round. And language itself depends on the individual imagination to overcome the ambiguities of mere signs. These two powerful speakers discover, however, that they live in a context; indeed their stance courts response from the world at large.

It is here we confront the trickiest part of Eliot's vision, which has for so long been treated as positing something like the determinism of society, or external fact. Characters like Adam, Felix, Dorothea, and in a slightly different way Gwendolen, find their freedom to do what they will limited by the external context of society and history. For some reason critics have often thought Eliot to be on the side of restraint and defeat of vital energy, simply because she is realistic enough to see that such energy is often defeated, or that a single swallow does not make a summer. The truth, of course, is that she believes in the creative imagination as the only thing that will revitalise language and in revitalised language as the only thing that will make life in society possible. She shows again and again, however, that the significant action of her most active characters comes to grief because the scene of their action is not big enough or appropriate enough for them. The stress in the passage at the end of *Middlemarch* is on the need for creating new circumstances that will make significant action more likely:

> For there is no creature whose inward being is so strong that it is not greatly determined by what lies outside it. A new Theresa will hardly have the opportunity of reforming a conventual life, any more than a new Antigone will spend her heroic piety in daring all for the sake of a brother's burial: *the medium in which their ardent deeds took shape* is for ever gone. *But we insignificant* people with our daily words and acts are preparing the lives of many Dorotheas, some of which may present a far sadder sacrifice than that of the Dorothea whose story we know.[25]

The first medium in which Eliot's heroes act is the medium of language; she then goes on to test the extent to which action in language—the field of her own action after all—can change the world. Society, it turns out, is generally unresponsive to the subtle nuances of language that trace the pathways of the mind. Such heroes of the word, that is to say, court misunderstanding. Nevertheless they must act. Felix, in the midst of the riot at the election is characteristic:

Felix was perfectly conscious that he was in the midst of a tangled business. But he had chiefly before his imagination the horrors that might come if the mass of wild chaotic desires and impulses around him were not diverted from any further attack on places where they would get in the midst of intoxicating and inflammable materials. It was not a moment in which a spirit like his could *calculate the effect of misunderstanding as to himself*: nature never makes men who are at once energetically sympathetic and minutely calculating.[26]

Nature may not, but art does, and calls them novelists. Felix can only do what he can; the trial that results is not due to his rash attempt at significant action, but to the inability of society to interpret correctly.

Society pays attention only to the neck-bands and strings of our vesture rather than to the spirit. Mr Lyons' daughter Esther, and her temporary wooer Harold Transome, represent the deficiency of this social attitude. Esther undergoes a process of deepening, however, and learns both how to read and act more significantly. Unlike her father, Esther cannot accept Felix's direct speech, because she is 'a critic of words'.[27] She is given to 'niceties'. Her reading is *Rene* and Byron, works that promulgate a doctrine of 'idle suffering' according to Felix, rather than 'beneficent activity'.[28] Characteristically, for this type of character, she is clothes-conscious and apparently indulges in 'unbecoming expenditure on her gloves, shoes, and hosiery'.[29] She has 'excited a passion in two young Dissenting breasts that were clad in the best style of Treby waistcoat—a garment which at that period displayed much design both in the stuff and in the wearer'.[30] Faced with the inheritance of a fortune and a proposal from Harold Transome, she is in danger of finding herself 'in silken bondage that arrested all motive, and was nothing better than a well-cushioned despair'.[31]

Harold is a man of superficial and hedonistic manner: 'His very good-nature was unsympathetic: it never came from any thorough understanding or deep respect for what was in the mind of the person he obliged or indulged . . .'.[32] He rejects the possibility of creative action and enunciates a philosophy of passivity: 'what a man means usually depends on what happens'.[33] Not, that is to say, on what he *does*. Like the passive romantic heroes that Esther reads about, Harold may be superficially attractive but his essential passivity is dangerous because it kills off the power of language. He engages Esther in 'love-talk': 'Hitherto Esther's acquaintance with Oriental love was derived chiefly from Byronic poems, and this had not sufficed to adjust her mind to a new story, where the Giaour concerned was giving her his arm. *She was unable to speak* . . .'.[34] As she becomes 'more passive to his attentions' she is about to begin to 'adjust her wishes to a life of middling delights, overhung with the *languorous haziness of motiveless ease, where poetry was only literature*, and the fine ideas had to be taken down from the shelves of the library when her husband's back was turned'.[35]

Esther, however, has begun to have her depths awakened under the influence of Felix, so much so that she begins to give up reading for writing: 'Esther found it impossible to read in these days; her life was a book which she seemed herself to be constructing—trying to make character clear before her, and looking into the ways of destiny.'[36] At Felix's trial she commits herself by actively and publicly speaking out on his behalf:

> There was something so naive and beautiful in this action of Esther's, that it conquered every low or petty suggestion even in the commonest minds. The three men in that assembly who knew her best—even her father and Felix Holt—felt a thrill of surprise mingling with their admiration. This bright, delicate, beautiful-shaped thing that seemed most like a toy or ornament—some hand had touched the chords, and there came forth music that brought tears. Half a year before, Esther's dread of being ridiculous spread over the surface of her life; but the depth below was sleeping.[37]

The fact that she and Felix choose a life of poverty and uncertainty when she rejects her inheritance of Treby Manor is very important counter-evidence to the argument that Victorian fiction is the story of sentimental bourgeois who finally find a fixed position in established society. Esther has 'undergone something little short of an inward revolution'.[38] The result of this revolution is that she can interpret surfaces accurately and therefore live a life of more significant action, the point being, once again: 'But we interpret signs of emotion as we interpret other signs—often quite erroneously, unless we have the right key to what they signify.'[39] Signs, like clothes, must be worn and they must be interpreted, but the one crucial fact that cannot be overlooked is that one must understand the meaning *before* one will be able to understand the signification: a paradoxical truth of the imagination that we have come across many times already.

So Esther's story, and Felix's fate, testify to Eliot's own belief that imagination and love overcome the dangers of mere clothes, as of mere surface signs. Mr Lyons, however, gives force to the feeling that we continue to see as through a glass darkly:

> 'I bear in mind this: the Lord knoweth them that are His; but we—we are left to judge by uncertain signs, that so we may learn to exercise hope and faith towards one another; and in this uncertainty I cling with awful hope to those whom the world loves not because their conscience, albeit mistakenly, is at war with the habits of the world.'[40]

The 'albeit mistakenly' is an obvious sop to the Victorian audience. In his frustration, he desires that his opinions, and Felix's, could be represented 'in a sort of picture-writing that everybody could understand'.[41] This 'picture-writing' is what the novel itself tries to be; it attempts to make us see. The effect of such picture-writing is to awaken active sympathy and imagination so that as readers we too can learn to see beyond and behind.

By developing imagination and sympathy, and a correct attitude to signs, the novel works towards the reformation of society. Nevertheless, the chances for such significant change is slim, as Lyons suggests in reporting his conversation with the imprisoned Felix:

> 'We discoursed greatly on the sad effect of all this for his mother, and on the perplexed condition of human things, whereby even right action seems to bring evil consequences, if we have respect only to our own brief lives, and not to that larger rule whereby we are stewards of the eternal dealings, and not contrivers of our own success.'[42]

This is the point of transition to *Middlemarch*, and the passage is perhaps the most accurate commentary on the meaning of the story of Dorothea Brooke.

Before moving on, though, a qualification needs to be made. Eliot's meaning is that the human condition is such that even right action does not necessarily—does not often—lead to good consequences. Motive and medium are out of sequence. The medium is the motives, or motive-lessness, of all the mass of members of society. Motives can be aroused by works of imagination, such as fiction. There is a troublesome implication in this, however. It is that we must judge people not by what they do, or even by what happens to them—although that belief of Transome's comes close to the bone here—but by what they intend. Which is to say that sympathy for the underdog leads dangerously close to sympathy for the inactive but well-meaning sentimentalist. Clearly Eliot does not intend this. One purpose of *Middlemarch* is to overcome the possibly too-indulgent attitude to her heroes in the novels we have been considering. *Middlemarch* makes this correction and both Lydgate and Ladislaw, and Dorothea herself, are judged not only by what they intend, but what they can actually achieve. Of course, Dorothea's failure is finally attributed in great part to the corruption of the contemporary scene in which she is forced to attempt to act. Her attempts, even though they fail, may well arouse the motive for action in other breasts and in this way amount to significant action.

Middlemarch is the most complete study of action and of the fact that action is a composite thing in that it is composed of opposites: the agent and the ground, or background of his activity. This can be put another way by saying that action also contains a passive, as is suggested by the bit of drama at the head of Chapter 64:

> . . . power is relative; you cannot fright
> The coming pest with border fortresses,
> Or catch your carp with subtle argument.
> All force is twain in one: cause is not cause
> Unless effect be there; and action's self
> Must needs contain a passive. So command
> Exists but with obedience.

Mere intention then is not enough; it must be realised in action. Eliot's concern with the ground of action can be seen in even the texture of the narration itself, as is revealed by this somewhat surprising interruption in a scene between Lydgate and Rosamond:

> 'Dear!' he said to her one evening, in his gentlest tone, as he sat down by her and looked closely at her face—
> But I must first say that he had found her alone in the drawing-room where the great old-fashioned window, almost as large as the side of the room, was opened to the summer scents of the garden at the back of the house. Her father and mother were gone to a party, and the rest were all out with the butterflies.
> 'Dear! your eyelids are red.'[43]

There is an unintentional comic effect to this passage arising from the apparent irrelevancy of the background information. It seems almost an obsession of Eliot's that whenever characters are about to interact dramatically she provides the necessary background to make their action significant and realistic. Rosamond and Lydgate are two characters, of course, who regard the scene of action as a mere mechanical necessity for their own action. Neither has much insight into the subjectivity of the external scene, and therefore cannot count on reading the motives of fellow actors. Lydgate is for this reason destroyed by Middlemarch society and by the strong webs that Rosamond weaves. She too has judged Lydgate only by his superficial attractiveness, and then comes to realise that his medical studies are likely to infringe on her desire for perfect freedom.

Middlemarch offers a highly complex consideration of the kinds of relationship that can hold between agent and scene, both of which can be regarded as having active and passive elements. Dorothea begins by being over-active in interpreting the minimal signs of her surroundings, the common fate, it is suggested, of ardent youth:

> Miss Brooke argued from words and dispositions not less unhesitatingly than other young ladies of her age. Signs are small measurable things, but interpretations are illimitable, and in girls of sweet, ardent nature, every sign is apt to conjure up wonder, hope, belief, vast as a sky . . .[44]

Casaubon too has been guilty of misreading, of expecting what society expects: that a woman will not be wiser nor more active than her husband. Dorothea finds herself forced into greater and greater passivity, one result of which is a moral growth. She discovers that what she had regarded as merely the ground of her own action, and perhaps of her own success, has itself an active subjectivity. She learns, in that famous phrase, that there are equivalent centres of self:

We are all born in moral stupidity, taking the world as an udder to feed our supreme selves: Dorothea had early begun to emerge from that stupidity, but yet it had been easier to her to imagine how she would devote herself to Mr. Casaubon, and become wise and strong in his strength and wisdom, than to conceive with that distinctness which is no longer reflection but feeling—an idea wrought back to the directness of sense, like the solidity of objects—that he had an equivalent centre of self, whence the lights and shadows must always fall with a certain difference.[45]

When the ego regards the world as mere object, it eats it; and it risks being regarded in return as object and so devoured. Interestingly enough, this passage indicates that the active Dorothea has in fact been seeking a kind of inactivity. She has been wanting to fit into the pattern of wife and grow parasitically on her husband. She is not unlike Gwendolen Harleth at the end of *Daniel Deronda* who must learn to act in Daniel's absence. Dorothea's activity and independence may have been extreme, but they have not been enough. Her over-activity is quickly turned into passivity, partly because she has not realised that activity needs to incorporate passivity into itself in order to avoid being turned into passivity altogether. She must learn, that is to say, to accept that the scenes in which we act are not always chosen by us, and further, if we are to act significantly in them, we must not be blind to what is in fact in front of us.

Dorothea learns this lesson as a result of two events; the first is the one discussed above, the imprisoning marriage to Casaubon in which she begins to find duty turning into tenderness, and the second is the realisation, when she finds him flirting with Rosamond, that Will is not quite what she thought him. She briefly sees Will as a hypocrite who has 'brought his cheap regard and his lip-born words to her who had nothing paltry to give in exchange'.[46] The suffering consequent on this discovery is short-lived because Dorothea has learned a new way of thinking about scenes involving herself: 'She began now to live through that yesterday morning deliberately again, forcing herself to dwell on every detail and its possible meaning. Was she alone in that scene? Was it her event only?'[17] This new sense of drama and discipline which is itself a kind of passivity, allows her to continue actively to play a part:

The objects of her rescue were not to be sought out by her fancy: they were chosen for her. . . . It had taken long for her to come to that question, and there was *light piercing into the room*. She opened her curtains, and looked out towards the bit of road that lay in view, with fields beyond, outside the entrance-gates. On the road there was a man with a bundle on his back and a woman carrying her baby; in the field she could see figures moving—perhaps the shepherd with his dog. Far off in the bending sky was the pearly light; and she felt the largeness of the world and the manifold wakings of men to labour and endurance. She was a part of the involuntary, palpitating life, and could neither look out on it from her luxurious shelter as a mere spectator, nor hide her eyes in selfish complaining.[48]

This lengthy passage is important because it marks the degree to which Dorothea has been transformed from someone desiring action but blind, at least in part, to the externals of her situation.

At the beginning of the novel she is in clear contrast with her sister Celia (whose name suggests blindness). Celia is seldom taken by surprise, we learn: 'her marvellous quickness in observing a certain order of signs generally preparing her to expect such outward events *as she had an interest in.*'[49] Dorothea has an inward light, but is blind to surfaces, and Celia is the opposite. By the end of the novel, Dorothea has received an access of grace; further light is coming in from outside and she is looking out on the scene not as a spectator of the picturesque. Instead she is reading the scene as if it were ground she could enter as an agent. Immediately she comes to this realisation of her own 'passivity', she becomes capable of action and changes her clothes to signal her new condition of agency:

Dorothea wished to acknowledge that she had not the less an active life before her because she had buried a private joy; and the tradition that fresh garments belonged to all initiation, haunting her mind, made her grasp after even that slight outward help towards calm resolve. For the resolve was not easy . . .[50]

The power of her internal resources soon takes over, however, and when she confronts Rosamond soon after, she takes off her gloves 'from an impulse which she could never resist when she wanted a sense of freedom'.[51] On an earlier occasion she is persuaded by Celia to take off her mourning cap and this signals the beginning of her freedom from the grasp of Casaubon. The cap had 'become a sort of shell'.[52]

Casaubon has been so often discussed, indeed so has the whole novel, that one need only note one or two items of relevance to our theme. One is his highly formal speech, which is like that of a diplomatic envoy or public clerk. This is particularly noticeable in the letter he sends to Dorothea and the narrator emphasises Dorothea's inability to interpret signs because of her intense desire to read into the external world what she wishes to find there. He speaks of her fitness to supply a need in his life and, because she cannot interpret the cold tone, she is unable 'to look at it critically as a profession of love'.[53] There is no warm personality in Casaubon; he is public, like a signpost. Sir James suggests he may be 'a sort of parchment code'[54] and Mrs Cadwallader says that somebody put a drop of his blood 'under a magnifying glass, and it was all semicolons and parentheses'.[55] This man, whose emblem is three cuttlefish sable and a commentator rampant, is himself a mere shell and characteristically he tries to teach

Dorothea only the surface of things and not the meaning. There is, of course, no meaning in his own studies and in the studies she undertakes for him she is, he believes, 'learning to read the characters simply'[56] and not the sense.

Ironically, Dorothea learns to read her husband's 'character', but luckily for him she also learns 'to read the signs of her husband's mood'.[57] As she learns to read him she finds herself 'no longer struggling against the perception of facts, but adjusting herself to their clearest perception' and she seems to be 'looking along the one track where duty became tenderness'.[58] As befits a man who knows only signs without any real feeling for inner sense, Casaubon's dress is suitable only for restricted public contact, and does not facilitate contact between inner and outer: 'Having made his clerical toilette with due care in the morning, he was prepared only for those amenities of life which were suited to the well-adjusted stiff cravat of the period, and to a mind weighted with unpublished matter.'[59] Not, one should note, a mind weighted with unpublished *spirit*, which would be bad enough, but unpublished *matter*. Casaubon is not only a publisher of matter, he consumes it in endless quantities. He means to recruit Dorothea to help *feed* his emptiness:

> . . . she pictured to herself the days, and months, and years which she must spend in sorting what might be called shattered mummies, and fragments of a tradition which was itself a mosaic wrought from crushed ruins—sorting them as food for a theory which was already withered in the birth like an elfin child.[60]

As Casaubon himself confesses, without understanding the full implication of what he says, 'I feed too much on the inward sources; I live too much with the dead.'[61] He has already devoured his own inward sources for this theory and he is now beginning to feed on Dorothea's. Dorothea is perhaps a figure only too susceptible to such mastication; it is suggested several times that she is given too much to martyrdom and likes giving things up. As Will says, she has been brought up herself in a life-denying religion:

> 'You talk as if you had never known any youth. It is monstrous—as if you had had a vision of Hades in your childhood, like the boy in the legend. You have been brought up in some of those horrible notions that choose the sweetest women to devour—like Minotaurs.[62]

In a novel that is usually thought of as dealing with 'social' themes, the story of Dorothea is perhaps a notable exception, in that her story is primarily one of face-to-face confrontations. She is trapped first of all by her own too active imagination, then by the social institution of marriage and by her husband's personality. She earns her own freedom and acts most effectively on an individual basis, with both Rosamond and Lydgate. It is this latter pair, and the character of Bulstrode, that carry the social themes of the novel more fully. Lydgate is a victim not only of an individual, Rosamond, but also of a community: 'Middlemarch, in fact, counted on swallowing Lydgate and assimilating him very comfortably.'[63] The agent of this assimilation is Rosamond, whom Lydgate bitterly characterises at the end of his life as a basil plant, 'a plant which had flourished wonderfully on a murdered man's brains'.[64] Lydgate and Rosamond are typical of those 'ante-reform times' that Eliot describes in such a way as to indicate that she is referring to the dandyism of the Regency period, characterised by 'niceties of the *trousseau* and the pattern of plate'. True, Lydgate does not give much conscious thought to these things, but he does expect a ready supply of fresh linen and plate.[65] Indeed part of Lydgate's weakness arises from the fact that his personal energy is exerted only in medical experiments; in the rest of his life he is ready to don the costume society offers him:

> We may handle even extreme opinions with impunity while our furniture, our dinner-giving, and preference for armorial bearings in our own case, link us indissolubly with the established order. And Lydgate's tendency was not towards extreme opinions: he would have liked *no barefooted* doctrines, being particular about his boots: he was no radical in relation to anything but medical reform and the prosecution of discovery. In the rest of practical life he walked by hereditary habit . . .[66]

Such a man of adopted costumes finds himself readily retailored in the hands of Rosamond who 'had been little used to imagining other people's states of mind except as a material cut into shape by her own wishes . . .'.[67] Whereas Dorothea serves as her own Ariadne and finds a way out of the labyrinth and away from devouring minotaurs, Rosamond serves Lydgate less well and she feels at one point 'as forlorn as Ariadne—as a charming stage Ariadne left behind with all her boxes full of costumes and no hope of a coach'.[68]

Seeing life as a superficial play, in which she tries to reserve the most effective costumes for herself, Rosamond cannot help but devour the individuals with whom she comes into contact. She leaves herself open, however, to the fate of all shells: the external world will eventually break through and expose the hollowness. She has helped to weave a burning garment for Lydgate, and early in the novel Farebrother seems to be giving Lydgate an oblique warning about the way of the world in general: ' "The choice of Hercules is a pretty fable; but Prodicus makes it easy work for the hero, as if the first resolves were enough. Another story says that he came to hold the distaff, and at last wore the Nessus shirt." '[69] Rosamond herself finds the external world burning into her as Will turns against her and rejects her toying amorousness: 'What another nature felt in opposition to

her own was being burnt and bitten into her consciousness.'[70] Dorothea
continues to probe this inner wound:

> It was a newer crisis in Rosamond's experience than even Dorothea could
> imagine: she was under the first great shock that had shattered her
> dream-world in which she had been easily confident of herself and critical
> of others; and this strange unexpected manifestation of feeling in a
> woman whom she had approached with a shrinking aversion and dread,
> as one who must necessarily have a jealous hatred towards her, made her
> soul totter all the more with a sense that she had been walking in an
> unknown world which had just broken in upon her.[71]

A similar fate awaits Bulstrode 'who had taken his selfish passions into
discipline and clad them in severe robes'.[72] Eventually this hypocrite is
exposed and finds he can say nothing in his defence: '. . . even if he had
dared this, it would have seemed to him, under his present keen sense of
betrayal as vain as to pull, for covering to his nakedness, a frail rag which
would rend at every little strain.'[73] Here, interestingly enough, the community acts in the cause of truth and instead of providing a costume, it
strips one off and leaves the man naked. He cannot even find defiant words
in which to dress himself. Bulstrode brings this fate on himself because he
has resigned primary agency. He has not discovered the kind of passive
agency that Dorothea attains. Instead, he is very active in society while
remaining essentially passive within. He has given up any internal agency
for a fiction of external justification, and in this is reminiscent of Hogg's
justified sinner: 'He believed without effort in the peculiar work of grace
within him, and in the signs that God intended him for special instru-
mentality.'[74] Bulstrode carries on two distinct lives, and this division of the
private self from the public one, allowing the public one to be the more
effectively active in shaping the person, locks him in a train of causes.[75] An
exemplar of the Protestant ethic without rival, he takes signs of prosperity
as signs of God's favour. As Eliot says:

> This implicit reasoning is essentially no more peculiar to evangelical belief
> than the use of wide phrases for narrow motives is peculiar to
> Englishmen. *There is no general doctrine which is not capable of eating out our
> morality* if unchecked by the deep-seated habit of direct fellow-feeling
> with individual fellow-men.[76]

Bulstrode's rigid doctrines eat out his insides, and this makes him act in a
familiar pattern. It is suggested that because Bulstrode has given up so
much in the way of pleasure, 'eating and drinking so little as he did, and
worreting himself about everything, he must have a sort of vampire's feast
in the sense of mastery'.[77] Farebrother repeats the point:

'I am opposed to Bulstrode in many ways. I don't like the set he belongs to: they are a narrow ignorant set, and do more to make their neighbours uncomfortable than to make them better. Their system is a sort of worldly-spiritual cliqueism: they really look on the rest of mankind as a doomed carcase which is to nourish them for heaven.'[78]

It cannot be put much stronger than that; in Stephen Daedalus's image, Bulstrode is a 'corpse-chewer'.

Middlemarch is too complex and long a novel to be done full justice in the space available here, and much must be passed over. Enough has been said, however, to indicate that the set of terms we have been developing is put to significant use by Eliot. This fact has important consequences for the way in which we must view her work. No longer is it possible to argue that she believes in the necessity for personal submission to an abstract ideal of Duty. The whole metaphoric texture of the novel works towards the complete dismissal of abstract, external systems. The whole of the vision of society and of personal relationships is built on the analogy with language, which is a system of potentially ambiguous and dangerous signs, open to misreading. The forms are not cannibalistic if they are filled from inside by fellow-feeling. The analysis of action is highly complex, and yields a concept of what it means to be a significant agent, which requires a proper kind of activity wedded to a special kind of passivity. The novel carefully examines excesses of activity and passivity in order to arrive at this concept.

One must conclude that Eliot's vision is certainly her own; it is unique, but that vision once again must clothe itself in certain particular terms and that fact gives rise to our central complex of meaning and metaphor. It is not that one has arrived at a Key to All Mythologies, or novels. Rather, one is perhaps getting closer to the fact that there is a set of signs, which require careful interpretation, and attention to them will begin to allow one access to the vision that lies behind them. At the same time direct access to that vision directs one how to read the signs. There is no system for reading novels. If one reads them with sympathy, one begins to discover the extent to which a broad vision can embody itself in a small number of signs. What has become evident, however, is that the major novelists concern themselves with major human problems and, in order to convey their discoveries, they resort to a complex of metaphors which provides them the best framework for elaborating a vision. The metaphors in fact amount to a suit of clothes for the vision, making it accessible. We take a first step towards understanding the imaginative mind by identifying the way in which it clothes itself. Having done this, of course, we are in danger of being cannibalised by our own perceptiveness. The energy of interpretation must be maintained, and any set of metaphors must be used actively and not passively, to see if they will give any fresh insight into any particular work.

Before leaving George Eliot, a few brief comments should be made about

Daniel Deronda, because it does help complete a picture of her world and it offers an important qualification on the subject of separateness and community. *Middlemarch* sufficiently demonstrates the evil of the abstract web of society; perhaps it is safe to say that it does not sufficiently demonstrate the counterbalancing need for community. For Eliot the Jews stand for spirit, or soul, which needs now once again to embody itself in political action. The Jews from their position of isolation and alienation have been able to maintain a sense of the inner life and Eliot's point is surely that it is precisely such separation that is the first requirement for the development and maintenance of the spirit. The pattern that this separated spirit must follow, however, is that of Prospero that we considered in Chapter 2. Separateness maintained beyond a certain point becomes destructive if it does not become communication and community.

Eliot has Mordecai repeat the story of Jewish history, especially the persecution and the acquiring of both wealth and knowledge:

> 'Hooted and scared like the unowned dog, the Hebrew made himself envied for his wealth and wisdom, and was bled of them to fill the bath of Gentile luxury; he absorbed knowledge, he diffused it; his dispersed race was a new Phoenicia working the mines of Greece and carrying their products to the world. The native spirit of our tradition was not to stand still, but to use records as a seed, and draw out the compressed virtues of law and prophecy; and while the Gentile, who has said, "What is yours is ours, and no longer yours," was reading the letter of our law as a dark inscription, or was turning its parchments into shoe-soles for an army rabid with lust and cruelty, our Masters were still enlarging and illuminating with fresh-fed interpretation.'[79]

The most striking thing in this passage is the reversal of roles; the Gentiles have become the Pharisees, reading the letter of the law only. The Jewish scholars have pierced beyond the letter and are 'enlarging' with constant 'fresh-fed interpretation'. It is this ability to read the inside of things that makes the Jewish experience of separateness meaningful. As Mordecai desires now to have his soul embodied in an active executive half in Daniel Deronda, so too must the meaning of the Jewish experience be made significant by external realisation or else die out.

Mordecai denies the validity of the attempt by some Jews to assimilate themselves to the Gentile civilisation; they must maintain their separateness that far at least:

> 'What I say is, let every man keep far away from the brotherhood and inheritance he despises. Thousands on thousands of our race have mixed with the Gentile as Celt with Saxon . . . they all the while feel breathing on them the breath of contempt because they are Jews, and they will breathe it back poisonously. Can a fresh-made garment of citizenship

weave itself straightway into the flesh and change the slow deposit of eighteen centuries? What is the citizenship of him who walks among a people he has no hearty kindred and fellowship with, and has lost the sense of brotherhood with his own race? It is a charter of selfish ambition and rivalry in low greed. He is an alien in spirit, whatever he may be in form; he sucks the blood of mankind, he is not a man.'[80]

Fresh-fed interpretation must now lead to the weaving of a fresh garment of citizenship. The man who gives up his separateness and accepts an inauthentic membership in the established society is the one who is wearing the wrong clothes and inhibiting the task of weaving anew. He is the one who is cannibalistic, sucking the blood of mankind. Here, it is important to note, it is the one who will not work towards community, towards the wearing of new clothes, who is the dangerous figure. Bulstrode warned significantly against the evils of membership. Mordecai pronounces the warning against both false membership and no membership at all. One cannot be dressed in the wrong clothes, nor can one be naked. Deronda discovers this fact in the inheritance from his grandfather. Notably Deronda's inheritance is a form of literature which he must actively interpret and try to understand, while 'Grandcourt's importance as a subject of this realm was of the grandly passive kind which consists in the inheritance of land.'[81] Characteristically, Grandcourt is 'a washed-out piece of cambric'.[82]

What Deronda's grandfather used to maintain, says Kalonymos, '"was that the strength and wealth of mankind depended on the balance of separateness and communication, and he was bitterly against our people losing themselves among the Gentiles"'.[83] Deronda does not simply accept the past, he does not 'inherit' it; he chooses it and makes important individual qualifications:

> 'I shall call myself a Jew,' said Deronda, deliberately, becoming slightly paler under the piercing eyes of his questioner. 'But I will not say that I shall profess to believe exactly as my fathers have believed. Our fathers themselves changed the horizon of their belief and learned of other races. But I think I can maintain my grandfather's notion of separateness with communication.'[84]

From this time on Deronda is possessed with the idea of '"restoring a political existence to my people, making them a nation again . . ."'.[85] This early Zionism presents itself as a difficult task and Deronda's aims are modest: '"I am resolved to begin it, however feeble. I am resolved to devote my life to it. At the least, I may awaken a movement in other minds, such as has been awakened in my own."'[86] The novel leaves off with Deronda having awakened a movement in the mind of Gwendolen, and stirring her to action in a completely different sphere. It is perhaps safe to assume that Eliot's intent is served by having Deronda arrive at the point of embodying

his vision in words, leaving the question of nationhood open. This conclusion neatly ties together the two strands of the novel, and represents
Eliot's own task accurately: her personal activity is the embodiment of
vision and feeling in signs, and her end is the awakening of other minds to
activity which will result in the only possible community, one that is
projected from within.

The pattern for politics is derived from the nature of language, as is
suggested by this impassioned speech of Mordecai's:

> 'What is needed is the leaven—what is needed is the seed of fire. The
> heritage of Israel is beating in the pulses of millions; it lives in their veins
> as a power without understanding, like the morning exultation of herds;
> it is the *inborn half of memory*, moving as in a dream among *writings on the
> walls, which it sees dimly but cannot divide into speech*. Let the torch of visible
> community be lit! Let the reason of Israel disclose itself in a great outward
> deed . . .'[87]

The phrase 'inborn half of memory' is another indication that Eliot, like all of
the novelists we have been considering, does not believe personal identity
to be derived from external circumstances; there is something inside us that
seems always to have been there, as if we were born with a memory of
experience before we are capable of experience. The allusion seems to be to
Wordsworth's 'Immortality Ode'. And the process set out for this inborn
innerness, is one of active externalisation.

If Deronda represents an external, active, executive self for the soulful
Mordecai, then, clearly, Mordecai *inspires* Deronda; he instils spirit into
him. What Mordecai seems to do is to awaken a latent awareness in
Deronda of his Jewish identity. This is not too mysterious if we are aware
that the sense of being Jewish here is equivalent to having awakened in one
an awareness of one's own inwardness. To be Jewish is to be active-
minded. Gwendolen is related to Deronda in a similar way to that in which
Deronda is related to Mordecai. If we put the characters in the following
sequence: Mordecai—Deronda—Gwendolen, then they are in descending
order of spirituality, or mindedness, and in ascending order of activity.
Deronda is more active than Mordecai but less active than Gwendolen.
Because Gwendolen lacks an inner awareness that could lead her to an
awareness of others, her acting is merely acting. She is totally theatrical and
is quickly reduced to ineffectuality by someone who has power over her
scene-staging, Grandcourt.

Deronda's middle position suggests that he requires something from
each of the others. From Mordecai he learns how to nurture innerness, and
from Gwendolen he possibly learns how to be a bit more of a stager.
Deronda is not apparently enthusiastic about Sir Hugo's aphorism that
'"There is no action possible without a little acting."'[88] Only a few pages
after we see him lecturing Sir Hugo on the limits of such a doctrine,

however, we find Deronda making a loan of Cohen in order to make discoveries, having been disappointed that Cohen does not have a daughter and so cannot be the relation of Mirah he seeks: 'That unwelcome bit of circumstantial evidence had made his mind busy with a plan which was certainly more like acting than anything he had been aware of in his own conduct before.'[89] So he pretends he needs a loan and soon discovers Mirah's brother living as a lodger with the Cohens. Here acting is half 'acting', and it is effective. Now, if Deronda needs to learn how to be more active, this suggests that there is something about him which is potentially passive. His character is, interestingly enough, reminiscent of that of Fanny Price. Like her, he is in danger of being too self-denying, too aware of external circumstances.

Awareness of the realities of the external scene is a prerequisite for action, but it inhibits action if it becomes too dominant in the scene-agent ratio. The danger is that of having all of one's identity extruded into the external world. Just before the rescue of Mirah from suicide, Deronda is drifting with the tide: 'It was his habit to indulge himself in that solemn passivity which easily comes with the lengthening shadows and mellowing light, when thinking and desiring melt together imperceptibly . . .'. This easy passivity continues:

> He was forgetting everything else in a half-speculative, half-involuntary identification of himself with the objects he was looking at, thinking how far it might be possible habitually to shift his centre till his own personality would be no less outside him than the landscape . . .[90]

This is clearly a Wordsworthian response, and perhaps the poem of Wordsworth's that inspires the passage is 'Nutting' in which we find this startling comment:

> I heard the murmur and the murmuring sound,
> In that sweet mood when pleasure loves to pay
> Tribute to ease; and, of its joy secure,
> The heart luxuriates with *indifferent things*,
> *Wasting its kindliness on stocks and stones*,
> *And the vacant air.*   [My italics]

This poem more than any other perhaps, expresses Wordsworth's consternation and confusion over the problem of the relation of inner to outer. Here, surprisingly, the external world of nature is recognised, in a way characteristic of Hardy, to be indifferent and vacant. Nature in our life alone does live, it seems. For Deronda, selflessness makes him capable of acting for others, but if the process is continued experimentally too far, the result is not only the loss of ego, but the loss of a projective centre of self. Hence the following narrative comment:

His imagination had so wrought itself to the habit of seeing things as they probably appeared to others, that a strong partisanship, unless it were against an immediate oppression, had become an insincerity for him. His plenteous, flexible sympathy had ended by falling into one current with that reflective analysis which tends to neutralise sympathy.[91]

It is not perfection that lies at the end of selflessness; it is Grandcourt, and Deronda is in danger of identifying himself with that piece of cambric:

A too reflective and diffusive sympathy was in danger of paralysing in him that indignation against wrong and that selectness of fellowship which are the conditions of moral force; and . . . what he most longed for was either some external event, or some inward light, that would urge him into a definite line of action, and compress his wandering energy.[92]

He does, of course, discover the inward light as it is shone by Mordecai, and so discovers what Klesmer calls an 'inward vocation' which is better than 'donning the life as a livery'[93] (his comments are to Gwendolen, but are applicable to Deronda as well). The subsequent discovery of his Jewish birth is possibly an awkward piece of plotting in the novel, but the very awkwardness of it indicates the importance that Eliot attaches to the proper sequence: one must first discover an inner vocation, and then the necessary external scene appropriate to acting out that sense of vocation will present itself. Gwendolen makes the mistake of choosing a scene in order to allow that to dictate how her life should be acted out. Her social shell paralyses her, and it is penetrated only by the burning words of Lydia Glasher and Deronda. The words eat through her shell and the sense of guilt within 'had wakened something like a new soul' in her. The effect of penetration from without is to give Gwendolen a chance of rebirth; she comes, however, to rely too heavily on the external support of Deronda, who becomes an 'outer conscience' for her. It is this displacement of inner and outer that is to be corrected by the necessary separation from Deronda and the isolation will perhaps complete the development of soul in Gwendolen. Deronda's capacity for significant activity arises from the fact that he has been capable of passivity and is therefore perceptive of his surroundings, of what could be called the fabric of life. Gwendolen has lived for too long only in the fabric without being able to see beyond it.

After this brief consideration of the last of her novels—which has not touched on all of the ramifications of the themes of acting, particularly dramatic acting as it concerns Mirah, Gwendolen, Daniel's mother and even Grandcourt, who is referred to as an 'actress'—what seems astonishing is that a picture of George Eliot as a stodgy and repressive Victorian could ever have gained any currency in the popular mind. That she is not an easy writer there is no doubt; just as there is no doubt that she is a vital and important one. Recently, just before his death, Lionel Trilling addressed himself to the question, 'Why do We Read Jane Austen?', which could be asked also of Eliot. Whatever the answer, it must at least include some mention of the fact that her novels lead us into a profound and stimulating experience of the mind and heart dealing with central human issues: the spirit and its realisation in time; the nature of communication and the possibility of misinterpretation; the nature of action and the dialectical relationship of action and passion. Also, one should draw attention to her relentlessly realistic awareness that the external impinges on subjectivity constantly. What makes this 'realism' important is the way she meets it. One way of putting it would be to say that she again and again points to the 'significance' of the external situation to individual action; and then she reminds us of the overriding 'meaning' of human motivation which finds its completion in vital activity. Another way of pointing to the essence of her vision is to think again of the line from *Middlemarch*: 'We are on a perilous margin when we begin to look passively at our future selves, and see our own figures led with dull consent into insipid misdoing and shabby achievement.'[94] The fact that we can ever find ourselves on this perilous margin is evidence of our freedom, and the evidence of this novel, as of all the ones we have considered, enjoins upon us a full, free and active participation in life.

7 Conclusion

> But the mere looking at a thing is of no use whatsoever. Looking at a thing
> gradually merges into contemplation, contemplation into thinking, thinking is
> establishing connections, and thus it is possible to say that any attentive glance
> which we cast on the world is an act of theorizing.
>
> Goethe, *Theory of Colours*

If the construction of a structuralist theory of fiction were the main aim of
this book it would now become necessary to trace our patterns throughout
the twentieth century. For many reasons it is desirable to avoid the temptation to allow an attentive glance to become an obsessive and never-ending
staring. The briefest of glances at modern fiction will have to serve and so
allow us to deal in a more general way with one or two important implications of the method we have been employing. Since the word modern
conveys for us a sense of historical discontinuity, any theory that tried to
find continuities with previous fiction would be a foolhardy theory indeed.
Nevertheless, such continuities may be found. Our argument has not been
that significant patterns can of necessity be found in all fiction. We have
found, instead, evidence of a recurrent active human spirit searching for the
means of significant action. The dominant mode of irony of our time
perhaps suggests that instances of successful significant action in fiction
will be few. If, unlike the Romantics, we cannot quite believe in nature as our
scene, nor, unlike the Victorians, can we act in society, then it may be that
the only realm of significant action left to us is language itself. Hence the
preponderance in our time of highly achieved and important works of
structure in language whose message is precisely that significant action on
any stage other than language is impossible. For this reason (amongst
others) we find that the writer or the poet is the hero figure of modern
literature. Interestingly enough, we note that from Shakespeare on the
theme of fiction that has been subject to our attentive glance has insisted
that Nature and Society only become scenes for significant action when
humanity becomes significantly active in the primal scene of language. To
this extent, then, it can be argued that the task of literature is one and
continuous.

One fact of life of modern history is that the individual has increasingly
perceived himself as subject to his scene. The scene–agent ratio has shifted
in favour of context. There are many ways of accounting for this. One is to
note the historical emergence of a new kind of awareness: the 'objective'
scientific awareness, or positivism. For the positivist, the real is what is 'out

there' and observable. Everything that is not observable, including individual subjectivity and meaning, is therefore not real. The meaningful is whatever can be expressed in discursive language and the true is not the good nor beautiful but the verifiable. For the positivist, the structure of the observable is structured by itself, by means of rules of its own. The structures of nature and society and language have nothing to do with individual agency. If human subjectivity and spirit have any role at all, it is the role of perceiver or thinker, not doer. So the overwhelming focus on scene deprives us of agency. The extent to which this attitude permeates our thought is perhaps evidenced by the fact that it is necessary to write a book to demonstrate that the history of the novel is a history of individual human agency in the act of achieving structure. One also notes that the dominant method and dearest dream of literary criticism has been to establish itself as a science and so gain respectability. This 'close reading' of texts is implicitly an inductive method. One understands a book by means of collecting innumerable bits of evidence and adding them up to the 'meaning' of the book. By this method a reader may *find* meanings, but he does not actively participate in creating them.

Arguments about the origin of the novel are, of course, notoriously treacherous things. Without venturing on either argument or proof, one might simply notice that the genre (novel) arises coincidentally with two important cultural events or phenomena. The first we noticed in Chapter 1: the novel arises as the drama declines, and in a sense 'takes over' one important function of the drama. The other phenomenon is the appearance of the positivist or 'onlooker' consciousness, that takes only the observable to be real. Now, a naive understanding of the nature of novels suggests that they are concerned to mirror the real, the observable. Hence the numerous attempts to define 'realism in the novel'. Because of this easy way with concepts of the novel, we have had to account for the Modern 'break' with realism and an increasing focus on the inner world, as evidenced in the so-called 'stream-of-consciousness' novel. As we have already seen, it is erroneous to suggest that in its history the novel shows any tendency to forsake the mysterious unseen for the world of the observable. It is not, after all, necessary to assume that a literary genre will necessarily 'reflect' a dominant attitude, or even an emergent dominant attitude. Poets are certainly the antennae of the race; but they are antennae and not litmus paper. A literary genre may well, then, run counter to a dominant mode of awareness, 'for the misapprehensiveness of his age is exactly what a poet is sent to remedy'.[1]

As we have seen, the novel from its beginnings has repeatedly demonstrated its mindfulness. It insists that the observable sign, or clothing, depends upon the unobservable (soul, spirit, mind, psyche, intention) for its value and meaning. The task of the drama that the novel assumes is to show that these two poles, mindfulness and the observable, must not be separated. They may need to be distinguished, but they must not be

divided. Mind, or soul, requires a stage for action; it requires completion
and realisation in signification or symbolisation, which is the more precise
word. As positivist consciousness directed its gaze more and more to the
observable, the inner world became increasingly something of which the
only witness was the individual himself. Inner meaning becomes a realm
that one cannot fully demonstrate in ritual; one can simply attest to the
existence of inner meaning. Subjectivity becomes, that is to say, more and
more subjective as the split between inner and outer manifests itself in the
development of the modern world.[2] This split serves, then, to increase the
individual's sense of his own inner being; this is, after all, one way of
speaking of the meaning of the Renaissance and the historical appearance of
the individual. The very event that gives the individual his inner freedom
and independence and guarantees his 'meaningfulness', threatens to make
his individual meaning insignificant by cutting him off from any public
medium and so isolating and alienating him. As the split between meaning
and sign developed, it began to become apparent (to some of the antennae
at any rate) that coincidence of meaning and sign would be increasingly
difficult. It should be interjected that to speak of 'the novel' does not mean
that such generalisations fit every novel. Rather they define for us the limits
of a spectrum; any individual author can be placed on this spectrum, or
continuum (at least theoretically) by noticing what degree of confidence he
has in the possibilities of this coincidence of self and sign in symbol (with
the 'naturalists' at one end perhaps, and the solipsists at the other). The
novel (to resume the level of generality) is indeed the one bright book of
modern life, then. It traces the development of the modern mind and
confronts it with the necessary task of primary agency that will guarantee
the continuance of both meaning and significance.

When we come to discuss the Modern (twentieth-century) novel we can
recall the way in which novels have always made scenic considerations
secondary to the primacy of human agency. We might expect that in this
century, that has seen the triumph of the positivist frame of mind and the
virtual elimination of 'poetic meaning', the insistence of literature on the
primacy of mindfulness and agency will become increasingly frenetic and
tainted with hopelessness. A central, 'experimental' stream of modern
fiction has so far emphasised the creative centre of the imagination above all
else that it has been willing at times, apparently, implicitly to deny the
external world any reality independent of the fantasising individual mind.
We can sympathise with this as an understandably desperate over-reaction
to the positivist consciousness of the time. As fiction has been forced to
over-insist on the primacy of the inner world it has also been forced to risk
the loss of significance. Ironically, or perhaps tragically, the loss of significance becomes equal to the loss of meaning. It may be that by over-
reacting to the materiality of the time, fiction is indirectly capitulating to the
very forces it would oppose. The case is not quite so desperate as all that,
however.

We noted earlier that the modern writer has chosen language instead of nature or society as his stage. The very use of language is evidence of the possibility of transcendence and realisation. Flaubert's desire to write the 'pure' novel that would be about nothing is directly in the tradition we have been tracing in that it puts the need for symbolic action before what necessarily follows from it, action in the public world. Before becoming too sanguine about the positive values of language itself for the modern writer, one ought to add that if language is taken as scene, then logically it too can deprive the individual of agency if it is allowed to become dominant. *Finnegans Wake* is a clear example of tampering too much with the balanced ratio between speaker's meaning and the power of language itself. For some modern writers, the problem is given a further twist by the tendency to identify man's being with language. If we *are* language, then it cannot be our scene since it is our agency. The effort to find transcendence in language is like trying to pull ourselves up by our own bootstraps: the effort is both noble and ludicrous.

Samuel Beckett's work is the best modern contemplation of this dilemma. The centre of narration that he calls the 'unnamable' finds itself obliged to speak 'with this voice that is not mine, but can only be mine, since there is no one but me'. He is further obliged, as he says, 'in order not to peter out, to invent another fairy-tale'.[3] He finds that he can speak because he is crammed full of words: 'It's a poor trick that consists in ramming a set of words down your gullet on the principle that you can't bring them up without being branded as belonging to their breed.'[4] Having been forced to swallow this 'gibberish' called language, he does what he can to rid himself of it and it 'spews, like gobbets in a vomit'.[5] The unnamable decides in any case to pursue 'fairy-tales' in order 'to set about showing myself forth'.[6] This paradoxical relationship to language, rejecting it as alien while being forced to use it as means of self-presentation, is an activity of the same kind as Moran's who 'might just happen to be masturbating, before my cheval glass'.[7] The stage on which one is to show oneself forth, is after all a reflection of oneself, and although human being is in a sense divided and provides the sense or illusion of transcendence, one never gets out of the closed circularity of the fact that one's being is in language.

Nevertheless, the impulses to pass the time in fairy-tales gives rise to a series of 'homunculi' with curiously similar names: Mahood, Mercier, Moran, Mollose, Molloy and so on. The unnamable's activities in language lead to an internal spiralling, like that of Yeats's gyres:

I must have got embroiled in a kind of inverted spiral, I mean one of the coils of which, instead of widening more and more, grew narrower and narrower and finally, given the kind of space in which I was supposed to evolve, would come to an end for lack of room. Faced then with the material impossibility of going any further I should no doubt have had to stop, unless of course I elected to set off again at once in the opposite direction, to unscrew myself as it were, after having screwed myself to a standstill . . .[8]

Screwing himself back and forth (in the linguistic cheval glass), the unnamable gives rise to Moran. Moran is an agent in the secondary sense. He sets off on a quest in implicit response to an unidentified authority, and he duly writes the report of his apparently unsuccessful quest. But it has been a real 'quest' and it has in fact led to the creation of Molloy. Moran finds Molloy in his own head.[9] He cannot find Molloy externally because he has been stalking him inside himself. This leads then to the creation of another homunculus called Molloy who is a higher transformation of both the unnamable and of Moran.

Molloy is indeed a higher being than the others, or perhaps one is justified only in saying that he is wider since he is the gyre at its most unscrewed. Unlike Moran, Molloy is an agent in the primary sense, since he moves at the behest of an inner urging that is almost sacred; he is seeking his mother. His movements in the external world are ludicrously inadequate however, and we may soon get the feeling that, like the others, he too is travelling inwardly. Seeking his mother, he is seeking his beginning and we discover that his end is in his beginning and his beginning in his end. Molloy spirals back into the unnamable: 'And even my sense of identity was wrapped in a namelessness often hard to penetrate . . .'; 'Yes, even then, when already all was fading, waves and particles, there could be no things but nameless things, no names but thingless names.'[10] So the unnamable gives rise to homunculi, which are then ingested and give rise to higher homunculi, which are then ingested. Or the process is the reverse, Molloy looking inwards finds something unnamable which gives rise to homunculi and so on. Transcendence turns out to be frustratingly and comically circular. Humankind is the source of its own nutriment, but it never really grows into anything else, it never really gets anywhere.

Beckett qualifies the sense of language we have been using thus far. We have operated with a distinction between speaker's meaning and lexical meaning, such that language becomes a stage. Beckett reminds us that the stage, language, is internal as much as external and that our inner being is derived, at least in part, from language itself. This comment does not alter the relevance of all earlier fiction. Instead our study of the history of fiction gives us a vantage point from which to evaluate the modern dilemma as expressed in Beckett. It may be that without a conception of self, of personal meaning, that is prior to language, a life of significant action is impossible. The dominant modern belief that the self is always a function of something else, always derived from some system or structure, threatens to exhaust the creative spirit by denying it any ground for significant activity. What keeps Beckett, for us, in the tradition, is his including of something unnamable, something beyond language but related to and needing language even if it curses the words that get crammed down its gullet.

To be pedantically thorough, one could go on to discuss the function of images of clothing in Beckett. Indeed one could discuss many more novels on this basis. Given the deep and similar idiosyncrasy of D. H. Lawrence and Carlyle, one could develop a sans-culottist interpretation of the modern world based on *Women in Love*. One could treat Birkin's shedding of his clothes to run naked in the woods as the modern reaction to Victorian over-dressedness. A discussion of Gudrun's clothing and Gerald's mud-caked boots could be made relevant. One would have to note, however, that at the end of the novel Birkin is comfortably dressed, and this would lead one to recognise that his taking off of his clothes early in the novel is a symbolic act with a particular reference. Birkin is reacting to the over-intellectuality of Hermione who, reacting to the same thing in him, has just struck him with the paperweight. In taking off his clothes Birkin is signalling the beginning of a change of mind. Imagery of clothing and themes of agency would show at least as much continuity as discontinuity with such images in the earlier fiction we have been considering.

Our method, given the space, would allow us also to engage on a comprehensive discussion of Henry James, using the concept of drama, ideas of language and particularly images of clothing. The first thing that Isabel Archer 'must' do on inheriting a fortune is buy herself a new wardrobe of clothing under the tutelage of Mrs Touchett. As a result of this new clothing she falls prey to Madame Merle and Gilbert Osmond. She discovers that she cannot escape from her wardrobe and the demands it makes on her. The important point, however, is that she actively chooses to remain passively in her new clothing, because she believes she can be of service to Pansy. She behaves, that is to say, as a perfect embodiment of the meaning of passive activity. In her new position, she is encumbered: 'Her light step drew a mass of drapery behind it. . . . The free, keen girl had become quite another person . . .'.[11] She fills this drapery, however, with new meaning.

We might allow images of clothing to lead us by association to *The Secret Agent* and to thinking of Verloc's hat, which seems to have a will of its own and on one occasion seeks refuge under the table. It shows more sense than Verloc himself. This hint from 'clothing' tells us that there is a dangerous split in Verloc between his intentions and his clothing. Indeed the whole world has been perverted because of a perverted sense of agency. Verloc has allied himself to secret agency, to a doubly dangerous agency of the secondary sort. As the narrator comments, this is the sort of occupation that will always fail a man. Verloc, reminiscent perhaps of Miss Wade from *Little Dorrit*, is always looking for hidden meanings and as a result cannot see the surface of things. He ignores or is blind to the surface fact that his wife Winnie has a deep attachment to her brother Stevie. Verloc is so blind to such surface facts that he can blithely make use of Stevie in an anarchist plot. Because he has been foolish enough to believe that agency can ever be secret, Verloc looks always behind the scenes and cannot see the writing on the wall: 'There was nothing beyond him: there was just the whitewashed wall. The excellent husband of Winnie Verloc saw no writing on the wall.'[12] Winnie, excellent wife, is the perfect complement to her husband:

> Winnie's philosophy consisted in not taking notice of the inside of facts. . . . As to Mr. Verloc, his intense meditation, like a sort of Chinese wall, isolated him completely from the phenomena of this world of vain effort and illusory appearances.[13]

Given their mutual misreadings, one seeking meanings for which there are no possible signs and the other reading signs as if they themselves were meaningful and not needing interpretation, it is not surprising that their lives end as they do; Winnie carves Verloc with the knife that was meant to carve the roast for dinner. She makes a meal of him; her 'significance' devours his 'meaning'.

In pursuit of further continuities one might contemplate one of the hardest of challenges, the novels of Alain Robbe-Grillet, which seem to be based on the premise that the individual personality has tyrannised the fictional world for too long. Robbe-Grillet seems to be striving for the meaningless but significant novel by eliminating the personal element. One might be tempted, therefore, to try to find a meaning in a novel such as *Jealousy*. One way of approaching such a task would be to adopt our notion of the relationship of agent to scene, keeping in mind also the reader's relationship to the scene of the novel. The narrator is apparently jealous of the relationship between his wife 'A' and their neighbour Franck. What keeps the narrator in a state of suspension is his inability to determine just whether or not 'A' and Franck have slept together on their shopping visit to a nearby town. We begin to realise that the repetitious 'objective' observations of rows of banana fields and so on are really signs of the neurotically subjective state of the narrator. He has become neurotically obsessed with the scene because he is attempting to eliminate his own inner torments, and perhaps to keep himself from acting out his drives, perhaps by killing the pair. The reader is readily caught up in this psycho-drama and may spend endless hours trying to figure out exactly what is going on. The text itself, however, is very annoying after a while. Probably many readers have thrown the book down and said, 'Just who the hell cares whether or not A sleeps with Franck and if the husband kills them or not? It just doesn't matter.' And indeed, one could begin to suspect that that is precisely Robbe-Grillet's point.

It doesn't matter, but that is the kind of romantic subjective drama that our culture is in love with. And our fascination for that kind of psycho-drama blinds us to the same things that the narrator is blind to. The scene of the narrator's observations, once one looks again, contains a number of subservient blacks. The characters are at one point reading a novel about 'colonial' Africa. So the reader's fascination with the romance—which after all he can play out internally and so stimulate his own subjectivity—blinds him to objective social injustice, to the facts of colonialism and racism.[14] This does, then, seem to be one possible 'meaning' for a supposedly meaningless novel. Robbe-Grillet, doubtless, inverts the formula we have been using, but the formula is still very recognisable. The novels we have looked at so far have all argued for the necessity of inner agency acting on a real other scene before there can be evidence of significant action. Robbe-Grillet reminds us that the ratio can be unbalanced in either direction and that too much subjectivity degrades the scene. In fact one might, after such an exercise, be tempted to comment that the meaning of Robbe-Grillet's work is nearest to that of Jane Austen, who made a similar point in *Emma*. If he could recognise the otherness of his surroundings, the narrator might become capable of significant action. To make this recognition he would have to become more passive in his perception of the external world. His apparent objectivity is at present a neurotic and subjective over-activity that arbitrarily selects detail from what is available. Along such lines, then, Robbe-Grillet's work can be seen to provide meaningful continuities with other novels we have been considering. It is perhaps only by putting the experimental contemporary *avant garde* beside traditional fiction that one becomes capable of perceiving both continuities as well as discontinuities.

Robbe-Grillet points to a radical split between scene and agent that results from an excess of romantic individualist subjectivity. This inner world of subjectivity we have seen is the source of what we have been calling meaning. Our argument has been that such meaning will atrophy or be vitiated unless it is given significant completion; unless it is realised in signs. The neglect of significance leads by a roundabout but inevitable route to the loss of meaning. Now such a meaning for 'meaning' is still not one that is generally acceptable. As Susan Langer, and many others, have pointed out, the one culturally dominant meaning for meaning is that of the positivists: meaning is what is available only in discursive language. Meanings are 'atomic facts', or the sum total of scientific observation and material nature. Whatever we try to speak about but cannot speak about clearly belongs to an unspeakable beyond, to the realm of the metaphysical—and metaphysical has come to mean, under such conditions, non-existent. Langer carefully demonstrates that the realm beyond cannot, must not, be reduced to mere feeling. She shows that whatever can be presented in symbolic form must be considered to be subject to logic, to be conceptual and therefore to have meaning: 'No symbol is exempt from the office of logical formulation, of *conceptualizing* what it conveys; however simple its import, or however great, this import is a *meaning*, and therefore an element for understanding.'[15]

Langer's theory of symbolic presentation has many affinities with the ideas of Owen Barfield, who has already been of central importance to the considerations of this book. In a recent collection, *The Rediscovery of Meaning and Other Essays* (Wesleyan, 1977), Barfield demonstrates the way that meaning was lost with the development of positivist, or 'on-looker' consciousness. He argues that attention to physical causes, necessary for the development of science, was accompanied by a corresponding inattention to the meaning of events. This 'exclusive emphasis' became a fashion, he says, about three hundred years ago:

> What happened later, in the nineteenth century, was that a habit of inattention, which had become inveterate, was finally superseded by an *assumption* . . . that scientific attention to the meaning, as distinct from the causes, of phenomena, was impossible—even if (which was considered improbable) there was anything to attend to. The meaning of a process is the inner being which the process expresses.

It is this last sentence that expresses exactly what we have found to be a central and recurrent meaning of the novel. It seems necessary, even at the risk of repetition, to say that the novel arises with onlooker consciousness, and in its 'realism' shares that consciousness, but takes as its task the insistence that meaning is an inner process in danger of being lost. The ideal goal of the novel is the re-establishing of connections between the inner and the outer worlds. The rest of the passage from Barfield is worth reproducing:

> The denial of any such inner being to the processes of nature leads inevitably to the denial of it to man himself. For if physical objects and physical causes and effects are all that we can know, it follows that man himself can be known only to the extent that he is a physical object among physical objects. Thus, it is implicit in positivism that man can never really know anything about his specifically human self—his own inner being—any more than he can ever really know anything about the meaning of the world of nature by which he is surrounded.[16]

Any attempt, one might add, to read novels as if they were structures with no meaning, will have similar results. If modern critical theorists are insisting that fiction is meaningless, then they are operating with the very conception that will guarantee their being right.

These ideas about meaning and the relationship of meaning to signs have certain implications about the reading process. The opposite of onlooker consciousness is participator consciousness. The reader who is content to look passively at the signs will therefore be a misreader. It is necessary for a reader to participate actively with the mind of the author in order to participate in the construction of the meaning that is realised in the signs. Obviously, if there were no signs (blank pages) this would not be possible. Nevertheless, there is a sense in which it is accurate to say that a reader must be able to understand a book before he can read it. It must be possible for him to have access to the mind behind the signs in order for him to feel confident that he is getting what the signs convey. The more usual attitude would suggest that a reader takes in a host of detail and begins inductively to build up a pattern of cognition and that aesthetic pleasure arises when he sees that everything 'fits'; that is, that all the bits add up to a whole. The argument we are pursuing here would indicate that the opposite is nearer the fact of the matter. The reader, because of the nature of the human mind, makes some attempt to identify himself with the mind of the author. After reading a few pages he may have to adjust his conception of this mind because the signs do not seem to fit with his conception of this mind. The details do not seem to be significant. If such access to the authorial mind is indeed possible (we have argued only that it seems to be logically necessary, given what we have seen earlier), then the reader begins, once he is into the book, to become a participatory creator of the book. His aesthetic pleasure arises *as* he encounters details in the sign system—not after he has finished reading the book. To account for this fact of aesthetic pleasure as one reads, it is necessary to assume that one recognises already meaning as well as significance. So one is led while reading to say things like, 'Of course, that is just exactly the right detail to introduce at this point.' One can see such aesthetic significance, because in a sense one is creating the meaning of the book by participating in it. Because of participating directly in the meaning, one can see significance.

Obviously such a process is fraught with difficulties precisely because the mind of the author is mediated by signs. Therefore, every symbolic work will be open to misrepresentation, or misinterpretation. The fact, though, that there is a mind and a meaning there that we can all more or less get in touch with, accounts for the surprising general agreement among the various 'misinterpretations'. These ideas, whatever validity or even suggestiveness they may have, do have consequences in so far as they define a 'reader'. They eliminate two types of 'reader': (1) the structuralist and semiotic reader who will not admit the existence of a structuring mind behind the signs; and (2) the new subjective, affective critics who can find only their own minds behind the signs.

One should point also to another important implication not only of the ideas about readers but also of our consideration of fiction as a whole. To do this we might pick up once again the metaphor of clothing. We have seen a recurrent meaning in fiction through several centuries. In order to do this we have had to assume that manners and morals and social detail are the mere clothing of the novel. In whatever period it finds itself, the human spirit must put on the clothing of that time. To try to understand the novel, any novel, by means of amassing a great fund of information about the clothing of a particular time is bound to lead to misreading unless particular care is taken. No one would argue that we ought not to know more about the social circumstances surrounding the production of any novel we love. The error would be to argue that such information brings us any closer to understanding the novel. It *might* increase our pleasure to be able to create a more 'accurate' mental picture of costumes and so on. But such a pleasure is a dilettantish one. As we have seen, the clothes do not make the meaning of the novel. One cannot understand the inner meaning of a work by means of taking a look at the signs and assuming that they refer to social facts outside the novel although, of course, such a motive is available to any novelist who wants to make a contemporary comment about fashion, politics and so on. In fact, in reading a novel, most readers find that they already know the significance of modes of dress and social mores. The informing authorial mind usually makes it clear why such details of presentation are included. The meaning of the details lies behind and inward, not outward in social reality. Therefore one must conclude that any merely social history of the novel cannot take us a step closer to understanding the novel. Indeed such an approach threatens to turn us once again into onlookers instead of participants, active participants creating the meaning that we passively find in the text.

Notes

CHAPTER 1

1. For useful discussion of the way structuralism eliminates the element of the personal, see Denis Donoghue, 'The Sovereign Ghost', *Sewanee Review*, 84, 2 (April–June 1976), pp. 248–74. For a somewhat different point of view, see W. Iser, *The Implied Reader* (Baltimore and London: Johns Hopkins University Press, 1974). The point made roughly here is qualified somewhat below.
2. Owen Barfield discusses this in *Speaker's Meaning* (London: Rudolf Steiner Press, 1967).
3. From a letter to Thomas Allsop, 2 December 1818. Quoted by Barfield at the beginning of *Speaker's Meaning*.
4. Barfield, p. 37.
5. Brice Parain, *A Metaphysics of Language* (Garden City, N.Y.: Doubleday Anchor, 1971) pp. 58–9.
6. Parain, p. 14.
7. See, for example, his contribution to *The Languages of Criticism and the Sciences of Man*, ed. R. Macksey and E. Donato (Baltimore: Johns Hopkins Press, 1970). For a general introduction see Robert Scholes, *Structuralism in Literature* (New Haven: Yale University Press, 1974).
8. The argument in its most elegant—and, I believe, illogical—form is developed by J. Hillis Miller in *The Form of Victorian Fiction* (Notre Dame, Indiana: University of Notre Dame Press, 1968).
9. Quoted in review by R. Lattimore, *The Hudson Review*, 29, 1 (Spring 1976) p. 121. From Olson's book *Olson's Penny Arcade* (Chicago: University of Chicago Press, 1975).
10. *Middlemarch*, Penguin edition (Harmondsworth, 1972), p. 668.

CHAPTER 2

1. Davis, p. 44.
2. p. 45.
3. pp. 49–50.
4. p. 285.

CHAPTER 3

1. References are to the Riverside edition (Boston: Houghton-Mifflin, 1962).
2. p. 464 Richardson's italics.
3. p. 185 Richardson's italics.
4. p. 211 Richardson's italics.
5. p. 398.
6. p. 388.
7. p. 452 Richardson's italics.
8. p. 506.
9. p. 499.
10. p. 149 Richardson's italics.
11. See Mark Kinkead–Weekes, *Samuel Richardson, Dramatic Novelist* (Ithaca, N.Y., 1973).

12. *Clarissa*, p. 282.
13. p. 285.
14. p. 407.
15. p. 419, my italics.
16. p. 444 Richardson's italics.
17. p. 433.
18. p. 441.
19. Diderot's comments in his 'Eulogy of Richardson' (1761: see *Diderot's Selected Writings*, Macmillan, 1966) are an early indication of Richardson's success in this endeavour.
20. From the 'Afterword' to the Norton edition (New York, 1970), p. 234. Further references are to this edition.
21. Gide, p. 235.
22. p. 32.
23. p. 121.
24. p. 39.
25. p. 104.
26. p. 106.
27. p. 188.
28. p. 189.
29. See W. Oddie, *Dickens and Carlyle: The Question of Influence* (London, 1972), and M. Goldberg, *Carlyle and Dickens* (University of Georgia Press, 1972).
30. *A Tale of a Tub*, Section II.
31. References are to the Riverside edition (Boston: Houghton-Mifflin, 1956).
32. p. 145.
33. p. 7.
34. p. 122; first italics mine.
35. p. 388.
36. p. 513.
37. See pp. 493 and 502.
38. p. 417.
39. p. 344.
40. p. 417.
41. p. 418.
42. p. 418.
43. p. 466.
44. p. 224.
45. p. 155.
46. p. 220.
47. p. 228.
48. p. 208.
49. p. 215.
50. p. 554.
51. Penguin edition, p. 33.
52. p. 648.
53. p. 578.
54. p. 245.
55. p. 419.
56. p. 527.
57. p. 657.
58. p. 657.
59. Carlyle, *Sartor Resartus*, from the chapter called 'The Phoenix'.
60. Conrad, *Heart of Darkness* (Bantam Books edition, New York) p. 9. Page references are to this edition.
61. p. 18.
62. p. 44.
63. p. 84.
64. p. 9.
65. pp. 97–8.
66. p. 60.
67. p. 47.
68. p. 119.
69. p. 101.
70. p. 124.
71. p. 81.
72. p. 95.
73. p. 112.
74. p. 82.
75. p. 112.
76. p. 85.
77. p. 28.
78. p. 28.
79. p. 92.
80. p. 92.
81. p. 93.
82. p. 94.
83. See *Minor Classics of Nineteenth Century Fiction*, Vol. II; ed. W. Buckler (New York: Houghton-Mifflin, 1967).
84. *Wuthering Heights*, ed. F. T. Flahiff (Macmillan of Canada) p. 106. Page references are to this edition.

85. p. 16.   86. p. 123.
87. p. 354. I am indebted to Ron Hatch, 'Heathcliff's "Queer End" and Schopenhauer's Denial of the Will', *Canadian Review of Comparative Literature*, I, 1, 49–64, and to our mutual instructor Elliot B. Gose, Jr, who discusses the novel in his *Imagination Indulged: The Irrational in the Nineteenth Century Novel* (Montreal, 1972).
88. pp. 356–7.
89. p. 62.
90. p. 63.
91. p. 204.
92. p. 295.
93. p. 346.
94. p. 63.
95. p. 75.
96. p. 5.
97. p. 9.
98. p. 35, my italics.
99. p. 183, Brontë's italics.
100. p. 116.
101. p. 193.
102. p. 162.
103. p. 197.
104. p. 175.

CHAPTER 4

1. Lionel Trilling, *'Mansfield Park'*, *The Opposing Self* (New York: Viking Press, 1955).
2. Marvin Mudrick, *Jane Austen: Irony as Defense and Discovery* (Princeton, N. J.: Princeton University Press, 1952) p. 159.
3. Jane Austen, *Mansfield Park*, Penguin edition (Harmondsworth, 1966), p. 448. Further references are to this edition.
4. p. 448.   5. p. 388.
6. Stephen Leacock, 'American Humour', *Essays and Literary Studies* (London: Bodley Head, 1916) especially pp. 86–94.
7. *Mansfield Park*, p. 455.
8. p. 53.
9. p. 442.
10. p. 42.
11. pp. 69–70.
12. p. 81.
13. p. 392.
14. p. 435.
15. p. 335.
16. p. 337.
17. See R. W. Chapman's comments on Austen's attitude to 'Improvements', in his edition of *Mansfield Park* (London: O.U.P., 1923) pp. 556–9.
18. *Mansfield Park*, p. 177.
19. p. 190.
20. p. 317.
21. p. 318.
22. p. 388.
23. pp. 390–1.
24. p. 119.
25. p. 327.
26. Without attempting to read an attitude in the novel, Marian G. Fowler in 'The courtesy-book heroine of *Mansfield Park*' (University of Toronto Quarterly, XLIV, 1 (Fall 1974) 31–45) argues that Jane Austen was consciously drawing on courtesy-books in portraying Fanny. To read the novel as irony leads one to conclude that *Mansfield Park* is Austen's demonstration of what happens to character when it is forced into passive, or spiritless, or witless (Mrs Norris) obedience to a code.
27. Suggested by Trilling in *Sincerity and Authenticity*.

28. See Tony Tanner's introduction to the Penguin edition of *Mansfield Park*, where he makes this very claim.
29. See Ramond Williams's *Culture and Society 1780–1950* (Harmondsworth: Penguin, 1963).

CHAPTER 5

1. Michael Goldberg, *Carlyle and Dickens* (University of Georgia Press, 1972).
2. *Dombey and Son*, Penguin edition (Harmondsworth, 1970), pp. 457–8. Page references are to this edition.

3. p. 865.
4. p. 239.
5. p. 374.
6. p. 307.
7. p. 619.
8. p. 435.
9. p. 322.
10. p. 308.
11. p. 281.
12. p. 414.
13. p. 283.
14. p. 447.
15. p. 363.
16. pp. 461–2.
17. p. 658.
18. p. 659.
19. p. 363.
20. p. 179.
21. p. 456.
22. p. 116.
23. pp. 808–9.
24. p. 111.
25. p. 786.
26. pp. 129–30, my italics.
27. p. 423.
28. p. 741.
29. p. 737.
30. p. 367.
31. pp. 473–4.
32. pp. 748–9.
33. p. 857.
34. p. 860.
35. p. 965.
36. p. 145.
37. p. 282.
38. p. 972.
39. pp. 165–6.
40. p. 95.
41. p. 96.
42. p. 406.
43. p. 208.
44. p. 207.
45. p. 107.
46. p. 219.
47. p. 140.
48. p. 297.
49. p. 881.
50. 'Symbols', *op. cit.*

51. *Little Dorrit*, Penguin edition (Harmondsworth, 1967), p. 881. John Holloway's excellent introduction discusses Carlyle's clothes philosophy. Page references are to this edition.

52. p. 191.
53. p. 285.
54. p. 814.
55. pp. 872–3.
56. p. 675.
57. p. 674.
58. p. 794.
59. p. 388.
60. p. 190.
61. p. 871.
62. p. 648.
63. p. 649, my italics.
64. p. 658.
65. p. 672.
66. p. 760.
67. p. 654.
68. p. 743.
69. p. 221.
70. p. 842.
71. p. 844.
72. p. 845.
73. p. 851.
74. pp. 850–1.
75. p. 889.

76. p. 863.   80. p. 884.
77. p. 728.   81. p. 805.
78. p. 730.   82. p. 570.
79. p. 731.
83. *Our Mutual Friend*, Penguin edition (Harmondsworth, 1971), p. 605. Page references are to this edition.

84. p. 600.   101. p. 396.
85. p. 348.   102. p. 454.
86. p. 760.   103. p. 454.
87. p. 194.   104. p. 154.
88. p. 584.   105. p. 303.
89. p. 53.   106. p. 256.
90. p. 69.   107. p. 104.
91. p. 62.   108. p. 538.
92. p. 465.   109. p. 528.
93. p. 475.   110. p. 688.
94. p. 319.   111. p. 637.
95. p. 766.   112. p. 796.
96. p. 609.   113. p. 454.
97. p. 266.   114. p. 749.
98. p. 704.   115. p. 427.
99. p. 345.   116. p. 591.
100. p. 454.   117. p. 810.

CHAPTER 6

1. *Religio Medici* (London: Dent, 1906) p. 14.
2. *Daniel Deronda*, Penguin edition, p. 787. Further references are to this edition.
3. *Adam Bede*, Rinehart edition (New York, 1948) p. 435. Further references are to this edition.
4. *Adam Bede*, p. 72.   13. p. 154.
5. p. 173.   14. p. 155.
6. p .19.   15. p. 541.
7. p. 304.   16. p. 29.
8. p. 138.   17. p. 119.
9. p. 138.   18. p. 180.
10. p. 313.   19. p. 224.
11. p. 176.   20. p. 504.
12. p. 256, my italics.   21. p. 520.
22. *Felix Holt*, Norton Library edition (New York, 1970) p. 62. Further references are to this edition.
23. p. 68.   24. p. 72.
25. *Middlemarch*, Penguin edition, p. 896. Further references are to this edition.
26. *Felix Holt*, p. 325; my italics.
27. p. 72.   32. p. 417.
28. p. 265.   33. p. 427.
29. p. 79.   34. p. 429, my italics.
30. p. 78.   35. p. 434, my italics.
31. p. 475.   36. p. 389.

37. p. 458.
38. p. 474.
39. p. 473.
40. p. 356.
41. p. 360.
42. p. 362.
43. *Middlemarch*, p. 384.
44. p. 47.
45. p. 243.
46. p. 845.
47. p. 845.
48. p. 846, my italics.
49. p. 71, my italics.
50. pp. 847–8.
51. p. 851.
52. p. 592.
53. p. 67.
54. p. 94.
55. p. 96.
56. p. 89.
57. p. 315.
58. p. 400.
59. p. 230.
60. p. 519.
61. p. 40.
62. p. 253.
63. p. 183.
64. p. 893.
65. p. 634.
66. pp. 382–3, my italics.
67. p. 834.
68. p. 334.
69. p. 218.
70. p. 836.
71. p. 854.
72. p. 758.
73. p. 782.
74. p. 664.
75. See p. 665.
76. p. 668, my italics.
77. p. 185.
78. p. 206.
79. *Daniel Deronda*, p. 591.
80. p. 587.
81. p. 644.
82. p. 48.
83. p. 791.
84. p. 792.
85. p. 875.
86. p. 875.
87. p. 596, my italics.
88. p. 434.
89. p. 442.
90. p. 229.
91. p. 412.
92. p. 413.
93. p. 298.
94. *Middlemarch*, p. 841.

CHAPTER 7

1. Robert Browning, *Essay on Percy Bysshe Shelley*. Elizabeth Sewell uses this as a chapter heading in *The Orphic Voice* (New Haven, 1960).
2. Already, and in the rest of this chapter, I refer indirectly to ideas developed by Owen Barfield.
3. References are to *Molloy, Malone Dies, The Unnamable*, as published by Grove Press in *Three Novels by Samuel Beckett* (Evergreen Black Cat edition, New York, 1965) p. 307.
4. p. 324.
5. p. 325.
6. p. 326.
7. p. 102.
8. p. 316.
9. See pp. 112 & 115.
10. p. 31.
11. *The Portrait of a Lady*, Riverside edition (Boston : Houghton Mifflin, 1963) p. 324.
12. *The Secret Agent*, Everyman edition (London: Dent, 1974), p. 240.
13. p. 154
14. Dorothée Kom, a graduate student at Dalhousie, made me aware of this. She found helpful the considerations of Frederic Jameson author of 'Modernism and

Its Repressed: Robbe-Grillet as Anti-Colonialist', *Diacritics* (Summer, 1976).
Jameson is reviewing *Lecture Politique du Roman* La Jalousie *d'Alain Robbe-Grillet*,
by Jacques Leenhardt.
15. Susan Langer, *Philosophy in a New Key* (Mentor Books, 1951) p. 90.
16. Barfield, p. 12.

Index